Untitled

THE DIARY OF MY 72nd YEAR

Untitled

THE DIARY OF MY 72nd YEAR

by MORRIS L. ERNST

ROBERT B. LUCE, INC.

New York

UNTITLED: The Diary of My 72nd Year

Library of Congress Catalog Card Number: 62-21200

MANUFACTURED IN THE UNITED STATES OF AMERICA

VAN REES PRESS • NEW YORK

Dedicated to Maggie

PUBLISHER'S NOTE

This is the second volume of Morris Ernst's diaries to appear in print. The first, *Touch Wood,* was the result of Mr. Ernst's decision, at the age of 70, to become a diarist. *Untitled: The Diary of My 72nd Year,* covers the year 1960.

At the author's request, his publishers took full responsibility for editing the complete diaries, selecting at random from the wealth of ideas, reminiscences and encounters Mr. Ernst set down in his diary for the year.

Any references to matters which must remain confidential between lawyer and client have, of course, been eliminated. As for the balance of the material, we have selected those portions which we felt would provide the reader with the most amusement, insight, entertainment, and information.

Untitled

THE DIARY OF MY 72nd YEAR

January, 1960

New Year's Eve, 1959

The holidays are at an end—Lord be praised. I'm always at a low when people are artificial. It's as if all women wore too much rouge and all men, no matter what their inner feelings, wore silky stovepipe hats. Possessions ride the waves, and things at this season are superior to thoughts.

I envy Maggie who looks out of our Washington Square window this morning and says: "You fool, you, what are you doing on a tree when snow is on the grass?" She talked only to a blue jay and herself.

So I'm weary—or blasé, or bored. Surely for the next year or decade or half century I must find new excitements. I enjoy most, and hence envy, the leaping minds—the hurdling ideas, the conclusions which arrive without man's ability to tell in simple words how the leap was made. Heywood,[1] the laziest man I ever knew, had it, on occasion, when he dropped into the office to borrow a typewriter to write a high-riding column. Russell[2] gave me my first best chance to explore the will-o'-the-wisp known as wisdom. Although our contacts in person or by his charmed quill-styled letter-writing were less than daily, I now know that for twenty-five years the challenge in my mind was daily, "How would R. L. approach the issue?"

And so I'm low because I'm in doubt, constantly questioning what to do with the tail end of my life. In casual fashion I outline a book on the Law. As editor of a series I'll hit some peaks—drawing up outlines, writing first drafts—but it's not and has never been my dish to polish, to rearrange, to rework material. My occupation has always been in the area of inventing and, on rare occasions in the law, discovering new and upsetting theories for clients. The lawyer is more than a propounder of law. There is a little used area, where the robes of judges glide off their shoulders, and they become semilegislators, discovering that behaviours of man are deemed to be Against Public Policy—a phrase inconsistent to the immutability of the law.

In the past fortnight there have been the usual series of pleasures. But these little waves on the waters have no relation to the following and enduring tides that have carried me through most of my adult life. I cry out for a new tide, an exciting new persistent trade wind.

[1] The late Heywood Broun, columnist and author.
[2] The late Russell Leffingwell, former chairman, J. P. Morgan, leader of the bar.

Friday, January 1

Leisure. Coffee with Armseys [3] while they ate breakfast, and then to another Bergman movie and a French cartoon. A good New Year's present. These show the potential of the screen, but as long as Skouras, Sarnoff and Paley do not care enough about this nation, and probably never see any product of the silver screen except their own, I guess the Lowest Common Denominator of the tawdry will have its will.

Dinner with Connie and Mike [4]—good Chinese food on 3rd Street.

Cocktail party at B. L. C.,[5] crowded, noisy and amusing. Met young folk I had not seen for years. A kind of renewal sensation. Some I could not visit with at length, many I wanted—after a "How do you do"—to get away from. Many of the young and old are letting life pass by them. They are afraid of rejection slips and don't know that vitality can atrophy, as do muscles, through lack of use. But the *élan vital* shrinks if not used, and is not used because of lack of conceit, inability to face rejection—not knowing that the goal is merely to have more victories than defeats, more pleasure than pain, aided by a changing panorama of desires.

Saturday, January 2 and Sunday, January 3

A placid week end ending with high, hot sun. Saturday at the office to open mail and ponder without interruption. Home to watch professional football with its wealth of decep-

[3] James Armsey, Ford Foundation, and his wife, Beth.
[4] Daughter and her husband, Simon Michael Bessie.
[5] Barry L. Cohen, attorney.

3

tion, dozing and letting my mind play. Old Man Calvin holds his dead hand over me. It's O.K. to spend time watching hockey (I wish the Rangers had a good team) or playing golf —and all to no purpose. But if man uses his mind there should be some noble, high objective. Satan makes mischief for idle hands; but Freud comes along and says you make your own mischief and destiny by avoiding contemplation. In a century Freud will submerge Calvin.

In the evening to Littau's.[6] Here there were biologists, barristers, editors, electronists (Is that a word and if not, why not?). Good talk—no answers, few definitions, but a stirring array of questions—with obvious displays of optimism and pessimism.

Sunday was grand in a tender minor key. Hot bath with my blown-up tub pillow, iced coffee instead of Churchill's scotch, the book review sections of the *Times* and *Tribune*. Just Romanesque and no soap or wash rag interferences. Front pages again tell of military leaders who are disturbed by our complaisance, a smarty pants review of reprint of *Hecate County* without a trace of idea as to why it was banned years ago and is legal today.

Then for a walk—only a few leaves on the trees. We go by the stone chess tables and see men who look like what are called bums, but I suggest bums don't play chess; dropped in for coffee at Lena L.'s,[7] noted the ugly yellow brick in new apartments. Why not red—more expensive or is it yellow to be different, or is it not red because red is more pleasing, makes the edifice more valuable, hence higher taxes? Changed side on each street to get the sun and so we strolled, me with my cane tapping every third iron rail or every other crack in the pavement. Some day I'll drop my cowardice and take my cane to the office. I may even wear my beret. I'll say,

[6] Mr. and Mrs. Alan Littau, lawyer.
[7] Dr. Lena Levine, psychiatrist and promising TV star.

4

so what? Let them think what they please. I'll live by my standards and not by societal conventions.

Maggie took Stef and Nick [8] to a circus. The kids did not like it. It was humans in pantomime—while puppet shows of animals are with voice. I understand and agree.

Nearly forgot. Saw my favorite ballet troupe, The Globe Trotters, playing what they call basketball. No grace to equal it, not even my admired Agnes DeMille's. These contests are without loyalty. I have no eye on victory or defeat—just on the beauty of using and coordinating the human body.

Monday, January 4

A party for Marie [9] and her friends. These are the minds that unbore me. But maybe if I were a social scientist I would act in reverse and find the observations of lawyers appetizing. As I appraised the dozen or so social scientists who came to welcome Marie I did conclude they were an odd-mannered group, and not as distinctive as other professional people of equal ingenuity and standing—for example chemists, doctors, lawyers, or even dentists. But as I said, it is still a soft science compared to the more compacted and defined ones such as physics, engineering, medicine, and so forth. But they are my girls and boys—them I can't do without.

Lots of items today. I got me a hair cut and my annual manicure. The latter is still a matter of embarrassment—too uppity, sissy and swank for a boy from Alabama. All irrational, for my hands—usually dirty from newspaper ink—do feel better when my nails are neat, even though, unlike many men, I do not enjoy being fussed over by ladies—for pay.

[8] Grandchildren, Stephanie Goldstein and Nicholas Bessie.
[9] Dr. Marie Jahoda, social scientist, wife of Austen Albu, British M.P.

Lunch with Jack Gould.[9a] A good mind with a sense of urgency as to the fatal misuses of TV as the great corrupter of our folkways. I suggested a story: What restrictions are placed by the lords of TV over the viewing hours or programs of their own children and grandchildren?

Tuesday, January 5

Big defeat. For years I have tried through Captain Watts, the great ship chandler of Albemarle Street, London, to buy a Welsh coracle, and today they write they can't get one even made to order. It would have been fun to get a home-made skin skiff to fit my shoulders and weighing nothing when hauled on the beach or over rocks. On the other hand, it's good that some items of man are not made for public use—but only for the use of the builder—no matter what the cost may be.

On the other hand, a goodie. I read that man blushes not for shame but for love of truth. We all can blush. Dark skins get darker; fair skins go reddish. Now when a male evokes a blush it bespeaks charm—formerly it spelled weakness. Women don't blush much any more in our society. But children, being truthful, don't blush until they are taught to suppress or try to conceal truth. So says, in greater detail, Dr. Feldman of Rochester Medical Center.

A gusher of clients who believe they need a bit of counsel.

And all the stenogs and office boys entered my office to hear me chat about England and the debacle of the dreamless Labor Party; Sicily with its hard rocks and (hard?) attitude toward women—a pressure toward male homosexuality; Switzerland with its amazing national ties despite four languages and two potent religious groups; and Rome with its

[9a] The *New York Times* TV and Radio editor.

6

beauties of Caesar and the Renaissance. Good questions, and I do believe everyone enjoyed it. Odd that the lawyers, even partners, never have requested such a session after one of my hegiras—even when I went to Moscow—or as a so-called Jew, to Egypt. Maybe my reports seem more authentic to office boys than to partners. Maybe the lawyers are too busy for such nonsense.

In *Hansard* I read a colloquy dealing with free batteries for hearing aids under the Public Health Service. How far ahead they are. And why does deafness fail to evoke even a part of the sympathy and understanding that goes with the blind who can so easily communicate with fellow men? And now the totally blind can *hear* ordinary print—by a portable instrument. But no instrument to date can translate sound into light and back into a sound sufficiently precise to get to the totally deaf ear.

Wednesday, January 6

Wrote Dick Nixon about the President's trip to South America and my desire to help—toward literacy through radio. I hope I'm called upon because in the State Department there is no excitement, and I have a fair amount of knowledge plus a feeling of urgency.

Penelope [10] says there is a study of thirty-six law peers from the era of Elizabeth and that a high percentage of these families have died out. So we discuss why and assume it is not because they were lawyers (although no assumptions should ever be disregarded). Answer is that peers married rich girls. Rich girls mean families of few children, because offspring are marriageably wealthy if the division of papa's estate is limited by number of offspring. So the inheritability

[10] Friend, who must be nameless.

of infertility existed in the heiress family stem. I add, compounded by small families in the male peer.

Evening at Bar Association as Sinner selected by the Saints for the annual Twelfth Night Party. Previous selections were Judge Hand, Harry Tweed, Judge Medina, John W. Davis and others of that image at the Bar. I knew I was selected for a different purpose—as Fall Guy. So the party went off with barbs and skits as to my peccadilloes, errors and even defects of character. Jan [11] wrote me that when Rabbi Isaiah goes to heaven he is not worried if God asks him why were you not Moses, but what if God asks "Why were you not Rabbi Isaiah?" So in clumsy, inept fashion I was neither what the leaders of the Bar wanted me to be or say, nor was I myself. I did, in this confusion, tell about a need for a sense of urgency and the demands of our Republic to have new leadership which cannot come from bankers, chemists or clergy or any other discipline but only from a regenerated Bar. I called for a loyal opposition to the leaders of the Bar Association.

To Algonquin with owner of hostel, Ben Bodne, and some lawyers, until 3 A.M. and then home to 2 Fifth Avenue with some of the Entertainment Committee. So it's like a radio program—evaporating into air by noon the next day.

Thursday, January 7

Mail and calls come in about 50/50. Many tell me—some with affection—that it was improper to nibble at the hand that bestows a handsome silver cup on me. Others were delighted that I was not gracious, polite and pedestrian and thus brand myself as one of the respectable old men of the Bar. Much comment that the skit put on by my partners had

[11] Jan de Hartog, author.

8

satire, bite and was well acted and sung—all behind my back.

Saw Dorothy Thompson at Cosmopolitan Club in evening. She was mellow but gave no evidence of reduction of her lifetime strong positions and feelings.

Busy at office. Since much was novel and challenging, felt no effects of little sleep.

Friday, January 8

Lunch with D. Melcher [12] at Harvard Club and real fun swapping dreams for books—both agreeing that Publishing Leadership has little nerve or sense of adventure. It's increasingly negative. So we talk about new processes, such as getting one copy of a book long out of print at 50 per cent more than original copy—that is $6.00 instead of $4.00; why there is a tariff on book paper and none on newsprint; fears of joint enterprise to reduce cost because unadventurous minds are scared by an anti-trust law—which is a fluid concept if so desired; use of local weekly newspapers and local small department stores in towns up to 25,000 population to sell hardcover books; effect of shift to non-profit-making publications; effect of Ford Foundation, particularly the use of profit incentives in the market place, etc., etc. Maybe I'll do a weekly editorial signed Optimist, or Glandular Optimist, to see if I can get up a debate—the precursor necessary to thoughtful conclusions.

To Princeton with G. W. & E. [13] partners for the afternoon and overnight. All but Herb, Jr. [14] went on the train for a relaxed week end of policy talks. It was my party and I think it had values not to be found in the office or any place in

12 D. Melcher of *Publishers Weekly.*
13 Greenbaum, Wolff and Ernst, law firm in which I am a partner.
14 Herbert A. Wolff, Jr., partner.

New York City. That damn telephone cuts down on calm exchange of ideas. It infects with a kind of urgency which reduces thoughtful invention. Urgency is good as a generator but must subside after the motors are running. Idling is the mood for human motors to match wits and spark human engines.

Saturday, January 9

All day we talk about Law Firm matters. Eddie,[15] Herb [16] and I were not too nostalgic and said little about the day we began, with Laurie,[17] in 1915, but without a prediscussed plan we each told in our own different ways about the great gaps between our four personalities. If we had not been at odds, there would have been no partnership. The trick is, despite differences, to avoid either government by strong man, or the dissipation caused by the indifference of similarities. Interesting things happened in this Princeton Inn environment. Some who had not talked out did so; others were subdued with troubled minds and had to be prodded. At times the debates were put on the table in more than tepid fashion; and on some occasions with wisdom and freshness about the old and long accepted—a contribution usually rare but of high value.

Home, nap. M. had turned her ankle and concealed her misery—thinking, and rightly so, that I am unfriendly to physical pain, even my own—or especially my own.

To Walter Frank's [18] after dinner and there surprised to meet a man who was really against birth control, was violent against Malthus, was not worried by population growths—and not on religious grounds.

[15] Edward S. Greenbaum, partner.
[16] Herbert A. Wolff, partner.
[17] Laurence S. Greenbaum, partner, now deceased.
[18] Attorney.

To bed reading a tender novel, after reading a delicious letter from R. L. and a thoughtful one from Bill Lengel of Fawcett.

Sunday, January 10

This was a good restful day. Mike brought Nick and Kathy [19] up around lunchtime, and while Margaret cooked some hot dogs which they brought with them, Mike and I talked over publishing matters. Later in the afternoon we had a wonderful visit across the avenue with Professor Jotham Johnson.

He's a great classicist and I was picking his brain to see where I could find statistics pointing toward the amount of wealth created per annum before the era of Caesar in relation to the number of people on the planet. I find it fairly easy to make a guess at the population on our globe, but I am troubled trying to find the annual income of the people. Jotham was very helpful and directed me to sources of information as far back as 25,000 B.C.

The most stunning item that I picked from his mind came when he asked: "Assuming that there are now three billion people on our earth, what proportion is that three billion of the total number who have inhabited our planet from the days of Adam and Eve or the beginning of man?" The answer was shocking. There are now on our earth 60 per cent of all the people ever born.

Had a pleasant evening reading *Abel's Daughter*, a lovely book dealing in gentle and tender terms with racial differences in the South.

Was disturbed by watching the Hugh Gaitskell-Norman Thomas-Sidney Hook program. This program of three Socialists and two non-Socialists pointed up very clearly the very

[19] Katherine Bessie, grandchild.

valid reasons for the defeat of the British Labor Party and the complete impotence of the Socialist Liberal movement in the United States. These three Socialists are only really interested in technique and strategy and have never quite dared write down in detail the kind of a world they want to live in or they want their grandchildren to inhabit. They still get into a lather discussing methods of arriving at a decent world; and the main method that they can't get out of their heads is nationalization which may or may not prove to be a good way. In any event it was a sad show. Surely there should have been an even balance between Marxist and non-Marxist in order to have a real controversy between the men on the panel. In this sense British TV does better than ours, because their panel shows partake of the grace, humor and dignity and conflict of the debate in Parliament, whereas our shows provide heat rather than light and take on the aspects of the most tawdry and confusing of our daily newspapers.

Monday, January 11

I had a wonderful lunch with a very forthright, honorable and confused client. Felt most effective because I was able by chance to put my finger on the very question that had troubled him.

But the big event of the day was that I decided to get a Dictaphone machine. I hate the Machine Age; I wish I could go back to the horse and buggy. As a matter of fact, I'm not afraid of my sailboat but only of the engine—which I use as little as possible. So I have to face up to trying to use a Dictaphone machine. I am going to give it a serious try, much as I hate gadgets. And this is practically the first word I have ever dictated on a machine. I don't know how it will come out, and I am interested to see whether my diary when dictated to a machine will have a different flavor than when dictated to Miss Gross or written out in longhand.

We went to see *The Tenth Man*, of which Caroline Swann was a coproducer. It's a good show. Most people were disturbed by a wedding at the end. It's a story of exorcising the dybbuk, done with much of the old Jewish ghetto humor. It has pathos and gaiety. The old religious leader of all classes, sects, and kinds, had an easy formula for power over man. He would create standards just a little higher than anybody could reach. By so doing he created a potential for guilt among the people of his parish—and as soon as people are full of guilt the cleric has power over them, because he can lay down the rules for the resolution of the guilt and can make people dependent on him for the absolution and avoidance of guilt in the future. And now comes Mr. Freud who says there are techniques being discovered whereby man can work out his own solutions and his own life. To be sure, some people may need to consult an expert who has been wallowing in the guilt of others and who may give a tip as to how anyone of us can avoid being smothered by our own guilts. And our own guilts are usually needless because, as I know, they arise in the main out of a conflict between the standards created by society and our own personal standards. I have been lucky; I have seldom worried much about societal standards, and I have my own amoral or immoral or moral patterns of judgment of myself—for good or bad.

Tuesday, January 12

Last night we wandered into Sardi's with Poser [20] and his beautiful-eyed wife, and some friends of theirs. I hadn't been to Sardi's in a long while and saw many friends of the theatre

20 Norman Poser, former law associate.

—recalling those years when we used to go there one or two nights a week to pick up company engaged in the arts.

Lots of little tidbits: We had a good time discussing the flow of people between Puerto Rico and the United States. I was surprised to read that last year 85,000 Puerto Ricans came to our shores, but 59,000 Puerto Ricans returned to the island. It may be that in a few years there will be an exodus, for good or bad. No doubt if we were able to assimilate Puerto Ricans into the culture of New York as we did the Irish and the Italians and the Eastern Jews, there would be no exodus.

In the evening we went to talk with Joan and Irving [21] and I was deeply immersed in the upholstery business for many hours. They are a remarkable couple. I can't get over my admiration when I think of Irving, who has never heard sound, even the rap of a carpenter's hammer, running his own business, dealing with his own customers, and for 15 years employing a hearing brother as his assistant. Being deaf is an infirmity, but emotionally he asks neither pity nor special consideration. When he sees customers he makes himself understood. If they don't understand him he interprets it as the fault of the customer and if necessary he writes down the message. He is an exceptional craftsman who cannot do shabby work, and every customer he ever had admires and loves him. Although he wouldn't trade on his deafness, the truth of the matter is that every customer enjoys giving him business because they get a little extra feeling of joy; they have done their good will piece for the day, they have helped a handicapped person, even though they do not know that he often looks at his customers and says: "They have worse troubles than I, but their infirmities are not as obvious."

The law business goes fine, and the spirit of the Princeton conference is permeating the office.

Read a great quantity of random journals, spent a lot of

[21] Daughter and her husband, Irving Goldstein.

time with Tom Christopher's exceptional law review, *The Journal of Public Law* of Emory University, Georgia. This is a magazine for lawyers which deals primarily with the future. It concerns itself with changes needed in jurisprudence. It discusses at length pressures within our culture that touch on problems of law. I wonder why Harvard, Yale and other great law schools continue to be primarily interested in recording the footnotes of the past, without real reference to where we go from here?

Wednesday, January 13

One event of a busy day stays in my mind: a long talk with an admirable and lovely Catholic woman—a person of great charm, integrity, consideration for everyone she meets. There is no child to her marriage. Her husband has left her. He is also a decent human being and a good citizen; also a Catholic by birth. He has fallen out of love with her, and she is clearly out of love with him. They both tell me that the marriage looked as if it had hopes of success, but now the bloom is off the peach, love is out the window and there is nothing left. They both agree that if they continue to live together they will become uncivilized toward each other, they will feel cramped and emotionally imprisoned. The husband has found a girl, also of high decency, with whom he is in love and with whom he is living. The girl has never been married before; the husband is desperately anxious to marry her. The wife in all good will tells me, for more than an hour, that intellectually she is being cruel and indecent and hurtful, but emotionally she is unable to let her husband have his freedom. There are ample grounds for divorce, without any subterfuge, even in New York State. So this lovely person, a devout Catholic, will suffer the rest of her life, never forgetting that she is being cruel, mean, and nasty to her husband and to the girl he loves. She knows they are living together in what, oddly enough, is called sin. And my client—this lovely, devout Catholic girl—will probably have lovers and affairs, be bored with them, confess them, and, each time, say to herself that she will never have another lover, knowing full well that she can't live without love and love-making. So we have a commitment to an act of faith and emotion, which will ruin her and do great injustice to the husband she once loved and still respects, and above all, will scar the life of the girl whom her husband deeply loves. I suggested that possibly we might use annulment which is the Catholic's poorman method of divorce.

In the evening I went up, because of my admiration for Ephraiam London,[22] to a meeting of the Lawyers' Committee of the American Jewish Congress. I never will understand sectarianism. Why should Jewish lawyers meet? Most of the lawyers present I am sure are nonworshipers. I told them I was a nonworshiper. It was an intelligent group of people, and people of good will and noble intentions. I talked about the acts of leadership of the bar, and I was most fortunate in having an old friend, Marvin Berger, a lawyer for the *New York Post*, present. I picked on the *Post* for my main comments because the *Post*, while as shabby as the *News* and the *Mirror*, is more reprehensible, because it is, or poses as, a liberal paper. A liberal paper should not report on legal matters in terms that make people think the law is nothing but orgies and crimes. It should not, as some other papers do, identify the lawyer and the client. And above all, I said, this liberal paper, the *Post*, is the most objectionable of them all, because a lawyer requires a lot of nerve to represent an unpopular cause—and the *Post* gives him rough treatment if he represents any person or interests it doesn't like. It became

[22] Lawyer, author.

perfectly obvious in the course of questions that there is great confusion as to why a lawyer should represent a person he believes to be guilty. Laymen all over the land still are in doubt about this simple situation, and don't realize that we are all guilty of one crime or another, whether speeding or leaving our automobiles unprotected on a ferry boat, or eavesdropping in a public place, or giving cigarettes to a minor, or having a love affair with an unmarried girl. Most of us could be put into jail for a hundred years for acts we commit in one month; and very few people realize that it is the duty of lawyers to represent people, even if the client admits guilt, because the important function of the lawyer in the defense of liberty is always to keep in mind that the sovereign, the state, the government, is the main potential enemy of man; and the government, which has vast powers, must be put to its proof every inch of the way.

I made clear that most people or most lawyers talk as if everybody is entitled to a lawyer, but that not everybody is entitled to a good lawyer. By definition the good lawyers are the executive committees of the Bar Associations. The rest of us are really not, by definition, good lawyers. We will represent people who are hit by automobiles, or people who are charged with a crime, or people involved in matrimonial difficulties, whom the respectable leaders of the bar disdain to handle. In a way I'm amused, because I have been the great beneficiary of the leaders of the bar. Seldom a half year goes by but some great lawyer, a man of integrity, high up in the legal profession, a real "leader," comes to me to say, "Will you take over this case?" I am not retained because I have skill that my respectable lawyer friend could not develop; I am retained because he is afraid of the press, of which the *Post* is the worst offender, and his fears are invalid. He will not lose clients. He might be kidded at the Country Club if he had the nerve to come out for the defense of

Margaret Sanger, or oppose a charge of obscenity against a book. He wouldn't dream of representing a homosexual or a nudist, or any of the people who are considered unpopular and off-beat at this moment of history. I have often thought that there isn't a single leader of our bar who would have represented Leonardo da Vinci, who was not only a homosexual but a bastard.

It was a rather silly evening. Except for Berger's arguments against me, I learned nothing. Afterwards a few of us went to London's home and solved the rest of the world's problems—that is, all those that hadn't been mentioned at the dinner meeting at which I spoke.

Thursday, January 14

One or two very interesting items were brought to my attention by Penelope. She pointed out that in the forty-two years since the October Revolution in Russia, the Soviet government and scientists have been unable to come up with a single major drug discovery. Every one of theirs has been derived from the West. She gives me, as reference for this fact, the President of Merck Chemicals. So it seems to me that we are really ahead here, where our economy is permitted to function, where there is a sense of urgency derived out of competition and where, if you please, we have the profit motive—in which I believe. We are behind, however, in the field where the President of the United States has been in charge. We are behind because we haven't seen the other side of the moon; whereas the Russian government, out of a sense of urgency, has gone forward on all space matters. It is sad that we are now second-class citizens of the world. We have the money, and the brains, and all we lack is the desire.

Another item that amused me today was the banning in

18

Saskatchewan, Canada of the film *Room at the Top*. I haven't seen it—but somebody should really do a study of the idiosyncrasies of different cultures in regard to matters sexual in print or on celluloid. In Norway, for example, I have admired the great victory of my friend Trygve Hirsch, the lawyer, who, in connection with some book of Henry Miller's, had the court decide that whereas the book seemed to offend the folkway of Norway, all that should happen was that the book should be sent to Denmark, because the Danes were not offended by the volume.

More applause for Paley [23] for expanding and re-issuing the great TV film on the population explosion. I didn't see the revised version, but Margaret gave me a full report, and it's perfectly obvious that it made clear (as the press has never done) that the debate is solely about the method, that Catholics are as concerned as all others about the increase of population, and that all favor controls, by one method or another. Incidentally, on the population expansion problem, I was talking to some sociologists, and the thought came into discussion, that with population expansion, man will have to invent totally new techniques for government. Assume that the estimates are correct, and that in our country we may some day have 900 million people, cities of 30 million or 40 million. How do you elect a congress for 900 million people? Expand our present already too large congress (too large for thoughtful debate) into an assemblage of five thousand people? Or have one representative for every 10 million people? Someone should do a piece on this subject, relevant to local, state and national government, voting, foreign policy. Will we not, with 900 million population, or even a 300 million population, have to revise our concept of fifty experimental laboratories called states—or maybe will we have to go into uniformity and in a real sense into dictatorship?

23 William Paley of C.B.S.

Friday, January 15

We woke up with our traditional attitudes and tiny ceremonies. Maggie turns over for a final snooze while I get up to grind the Shapiro coffee beans, turn on the oven, heat the egg water, get out the juice. Since I wear no strangling night clothes, I sneakily open the door to take in the *Tribune* and *Times*. By the time I'm finished in the kitchen, Maggie has finished "mopping that mug"—as we have long called her patient dreamy washing. At once I must drag out her dream —that operation of the subconscious which takes a few seconds to occur but many minutes to report. M. tells me of the big white horse on the second floor of our big house on 11th Street. A blind painter was in the room and there also was Ernie King, our shipyard friend of Nantucket. The horse was a problem—there was no hay, and food was needed.

And then M. made a great discovery. When a dream is near release, just before fully waking up, she goes back deeper into sleep—compelled by the need of closing up the dream, getting the answer to a quandary or solving a threat. This causes return to sleep because the conscious knows that only in the womb, where the dream was born, can the dream come to its end. So that last catnap serves a kindly purpose. And Penelope suggests this theory is not unrelated to the ability— rare, I suggest—to return in sleep to a dream of yesterday. Some day P. and M. must meet. They have much in common, and I'll enjoy a sideline stance.

Lunch with Herb Mayes [24] and Maggie Cousins [25] at Park Lane. I fell hard for Maggie C.—this being the first time in twenty years that I have sat to talk with her. She is my gal of the year—maybe of many years. Although she agreed with

[24] President, McCall Corporation. Then Editor, *McCall's Magazine.*
[25] Editor, Doubleday. Ex-fiction editor, *McCall's Magazine.*

Herb that *Touch Wood* did not suit *McCall's,* she was all too kind to the diary and gave me a title for a novel or short story —"Young As Springtime"—which she is. Most of my friends are as Old as Autumn.

To *Saratoga* in the evening. We were abroad on the opening night. Edna [26] has not seen it in New York City but would not go with us. D'Acosta did a beautiful production—no faults, no imperfections—a constant unvaried high mesa of beautiful sets, good singing, good dialogue, good music—all at a high pitch ... but a level pitch ... no pinnacles ... no single outstanding moment of tunefulness, of pathos or love or fear. *Saratoga* had too much of everything. If they had plugged only one tune, if they had not rushed into moments of love. . . .

After theater to "21" to meet Eli and Amy Frank [27]—old friends—with their attractive daughter Marcia, a girl who ran, as she had to, from the constant public acclaim and references to her distinguished father in Baltimore. Home by one—since the Franks seemed to be weary. Bored, maybe!

Saturday, January 16

Maggie and I laugh each morning at the most outrageous puns or weirdest observations on tidbits in the press. I think these moments are the peak of our gusty laughings each day.

Joan and Irv went for some reason to the cemetery where Irv's parents are buried. Steffie refers to it as a park. I like this terminology and hate cemeteries.

To lunch with Lael [28] and a handsome Florida-Yale law school senior. Happy for Lael who has deserted magazine

[26] Edna Ferber, noted author, old friend.
[27] Baltimore attorney and his wife.
[28] Lael Tucker Wertenbaker, author.

articles for books. She asked for ideas on her gambling volume. Suggested a foreword by Frank Costello—presently in Atlanta jail—and as a title, "Risk For Risk."

In the evening to Alan and Paula [29] and there with gay Mattie and Roger Hunting.[30] I envy Roger. He has not compromised with the tops of the bar and is still one of their pets. Talk good—home by one, reading, and to sleep by two.

Sunday, January 17

Lena L. gives a party for her neighbors, many of whom on Washington Place or nearby had never met each other. It was a most engaging group and I enjoyed most Lena's Swarthmore-student daughter. As always, I gravitate to the youngster—male or female.

Walked to the Bessies. Strong winds; though cold, the sun was brilliant. The days are already twenty minutes longer and we sense it out of our windows facing the Square.

Worked on office matters, tax returns, miscellaneous reading, a double crostic—the best of all are the ones in the *New York Times*.

For dinner, Edna came down, and we three to our favorite Oriental dining place on Third Street. Like old times—just us three. Edna in great shape, gay and full of zip. I guess because she has so much she wants to write—a cause for living.

Monday, January 18

Years ago I wrote a pamphlet for the City Club of New York with a section entitled, "Laws Both Anile and Senile."

[29] Alan U. Schwartz, law partner, and wife.
[30] Lawyer, officer of Bar Association, and wife.

I recall that I gathered together many laws which were on the statute books and had been long outdated. For some reason, it is easier for man to pass a law than to repeal one. For example, I discovered that there was a statute on the books of New York State making it a crime to discover Captain Kidd's Treasure and not report it to the authorities. There are also still statutes that make it a crime to eavesdrop, one of the pleasantest foibles practiced by man. Yesterday, I was standing at the corner of Fifth Avenue and 43rd Street, and behind me a stranger said to a friend of his, "I can't go to Joe's wedding because if my wife's dress is fancier and better than Bill's wife's dress, I'm a dead duck."

I got a lovely surprise today, a letter and a picture from Katherine Dunham. This dancing anthropologist is one of the great people whom I have met. Somehow society has never really appreciated her. I must see if I can find some foundation that will supply her with the retreat which she needs so badly and which she asks for, so that she can continue with her writing, and get a little relief from managing her dancing company.

I'm reminded by a libel suit of a client of the story of the original John D. Rockefeller who was asked by a friend while meandering on the Atlantic City boardwalk, "John, why don't you sue these bastards, they're calling you a thief and a liar and a fraud." John D. is supposed to have said, "Do you see that worm on the boardwalk? If I step on it it will gather flies, and everybody passing by will know that a worm was there. However, if I leave it alone, it will wander away, and nobody will ever know that the worm had been on the boardwalk."

Nevertheless, our culture is in real trouble, because there are two important provinces of the law where the courts are impotent. I refer to libel suits and to litigation involving the custody of children. In the latter cases nobody can win and the children are inevitably scarred because of the reporting of the suits in the mass media.

Good news! Man has for some time been able to discover the age of various objects by testing with carbon 14. But now I learn that we can know the age of rocks by the process of heating. Thus, we can date civilizations back 100,000 years. Maybe this kind of scientific knowledge will have some practical benefits for man. But, also, it is possible that without any practical advantages the greatest benefit from the new process is that man will get a better perspective on the history of man.

Surely, we are different from all other species primarily because we have a history, even though man for many ages never could record it.

Joe Ream of C.B.S. came by for dinner. Maggie went off to baby-sit for Connie. Joe and I had a few hours of the best sober conversation I have ever had on the problems of radio and TV. The networks are on the run, emotionally, and in terms of public esteem. The great men who head them will not be able to think with clarity and simplicity if they feel that they must do something because they have lost the public confidence. It would be better for them and for the public if Paley and Sarnoff would let things ride until they had a few placid weeks, six months or a year from now— at which time they will get a better perspective of the revolution that must take place in order to have TV a process of education which is entertaining, and entertainment which is educational.

Tuesday, January 19

Maggie guffawed—a rare demonstration for her, when I danced my impromptu ballet this morning. This has become a kind of habit each morning, and today I did a Telephoning Dance while nude and shaving.

Harry Johnston [31] writes me a love letter—nostalgic, and going back to 1905 when we first met, disagreed basically on all political issues and still maintained enduring affection. Harry retired too soon, I think. I've been in his debt since the first days of F. D. R. and the Bank Holiday, when he did the job for me of setting up the machinery for the use of scrip if necessary. In fact, we had an expensive lithograph stone made. Exciting anonymous days and nights, and Harry was great—though Republican!

High spot—with R. L. for lunch but this time with Harrison Smith, Jim Wickersham [32] and others of the third generation. Took Alan down so that he could see, watch and hear Russell. I know it was a great experience for Alan. Nothing in the way of drama—just quiet wisdom—a rare attribute of humanity.

Wednesday, January 20

Met Maggie at Boat Show. Saw changes in New Horizon Class which I worked on with Olin Stephens. We have sold about sixty and I'm close to the point of getting royalties on this boat suited for young couples who are worried, as with most purchases, about upkeep costs rather than initial outlay.

I must buy a new sailboat. I told Maggie the kids are on their own. She has a few investments, and it's good and proper that I haven't a single share of stock or bond. I should die penniless—so I will live in my earning power and not on it. I think I'll buy a Controversy 36-foot yawl or a Hinckley yawl. At seventy-two I may have at most ten years more of

31 Williams classmate, banker.
32 J. P. Morgan officials.

cruising the Maine Coast. A boat is my retreat—my refresher —my turkish bath. My only reluctance is that I feel selfish vis-a-vis saving for the grandchildren. The children are on their own. We threw them out young to make their living, and they have taste. They disdain the chromeplate culture.

Barry Gray called up—caught short—so went up to WMCA and conversed for an hour. By the time I got home there were calls—"Why didn't you let me know?"

Thursday, January 21

Everything went along sweetly today. Up to Trevor Gardner of Hycon at his hotel by 8:30 A.M. Good setting for conferring—he in shorts and dressing-gown, a proper garb to discuss the place of scientists in the tactics of Peace. I suggested that an organization be formed composed of great people—Gavin, Gardner and many others—who left Ike's Cabinet because of lack of vision of the administration.

Lunch with young men concerned with paper and newsprint as an instrument of democracy. I showed off quite a bit.

Friday, January 22

A busy day in Washington. Tom Dodd, gracious and generous with his precious time, discussing Galindez case and Cuba. Told him of Overseas Press Club meeting where Matthews of *New York Times* still excuses and apologizes for all of Castro's very apparent dictatorship trends. Then to Mike Monroney, who is hopping around as is the habit of most senators; to lunch with secretaries to senators; to chat with the warmest of cold-looking diplomats, Eugene Black, about South America and more particularly about making wealth from the bottom of a society through literacy; to FCC to urge a bit of calm in regard to TV since human decisions made under pressure or in retreat are usually unwise; to Democratic Club cocktail party for H. S. T.—saw many old friends—and to dinner with Don Agger [33] and his mysteriously beautiful bride.

Like old days when the youth of the government had excitement. Late plane home.

Saturday, January 23

All day at office but hopped up to Voisin for lunch with Ellen Doubleday [34]—beautiful as ever. What fun it was to dig out of joint pools of the past amusing and pleasant memories of Nelson, the publisher, about whom only the improbable was true. Must see more of Ellen, who with her kids has done well with her life.

Ike Heller in from New Orleans—a wise lawyer and a gallant human being.

Irritated by Benton-Gray dialogue on WMCA. Benton said no trouble on Quiz TV in England because his company, Britannica, gets paid to draw up questions for shows. Tried to get station on phone—no answer—to tell them of British mess and the retaining of Sir Lionel Heald by the TV network to make a report. Thus does our public get uncorrected information even from honorable people.

[33] Former NATO official, now lawyer in Washington.
[34] Mrs. Nelson Doubleday.

Sunday, January 24

Picked up Alan and Paula and on to see a yawl at Orienta Shipyard. Well found but not just what we want to buy at our great age. Then to Baron's [35] for lunch. An amazing guy—just selected by Wall Street Journal as one of the ten men of last decade most significant in terms of big business.

Beautiful day. Drove home only to clean up and off to Fred Nathan's [36] where we had a good tough argument re shames of the bar, ethics of prosecutors giving cash to those who help get convictions so that such persons will not be bumped off by underworld. Carmichael of C.B.S. legal staff, good argufier, trained as secretary to Jerome Frank.

Then to Rickey's Restaurant to meet a character who was convicted in Federal Court. I rather suspect he was framed—but too late to help much.

Very late to bed and worried about justice and injustice.

Monday, January 25

Matt Nimitz [37] at 2 Fifth for breakfast to discuss my visit on February 8th to Williams College. They want me to talk for an hour or so with prelaw group. Not too wise to get lucky old men to describe a profession to future entrants. We are too apt to translate success or happiness in our occupation into terms of ability and work habits rather than luck. Better get the lads who are out only a decade. Also talked of something similar to Telethon—open to students, faculty and townspeople. I'll start off, as he suggested, with Population

[35] Sydney Baron, public relations.
[36] Law partner.
[37] Williams College Rhodes Scholar.

Explosion, Censorship and TV problems and then after these three let the questions pour in—if there be questions. If not, it's my fault—as it is always the fault of the teacher.

Penelope tells me that in Norway, Betting Tax income is used for research and that the Football Pool alone has supplied over one million pounds for research. We can't do it here. Hypocrisy demands that betting be limited to tracks. For the rich it is moral, but to legalize it off track is immoral. It's like pornography; at $20.00 it is not attacked. It can't hurt the rich—already corrupted or incorruptible—but at $2.00, we must save the poor even though we ourselves of course can't be hurt by any book. Man always worries about the soul of the other person—but not for his own.

Home to dinner—restful and ready for a long night's sleep—after five hours at night for the past five or six days.

Tuesday, January 26

Relaxation far from law and public issue to read publications of my Amateur Yacht Research Society—which is so acutely run by Yvonne Bloemhard. The great new adventure deals with twin hulls—catamarans for cruising with ample living space. Next we will dig into a hydrofoil—skating on the water—for those who seek speed, always greater speed. Why this mania for speed—ever faster—to save minutes? Or is it the best part of the nature of man to attain the impossible—Everest climbed because "it was there." How do we get competition for contemplation? Can we develop standards and grades for the thoughtful, the contemplative, and have all mankind strive to reach such pinnacles of calm?

My best letter of the day came from a secretary in the office whom I retained to dig up Population versus Production rates for the separate continents. Here it is—a better present than a case of wine from a happy client who has paid me thousands of dollars.

MR. ERNST:

I didn't want to take up your time yesterday—you looked so busy. But you can think of answering a note if or when you have time.

First, was the work satisfactory and did you get the right information from it. I really loved doing it—it's been a long time since I've had a project all my own to work on like that, and I was enthusiastic about it—perhaps out of proportion with the importance of such a little project. However, I would like to know if you were satisfied with it.

I would like to do something similar soon—if you have anything you think I can handle.

By the way, I am using the money as a down payment on a writing course—at the New School, I think. Isn't it rare when one (not you, of course) can do something he really and truly enjoys, get money for it and purchase something again, which he really and truly enjoys and wants? It's a good feeling.

Roz

Wednesday, January 27

Connie is having trouble because Kathie cried her eyes out on her first day at school. Not unusual in the sophisticated part of our society. What happens in Japan when babies until school age are strapped physically to mother—does this tie emotional strappings? What in cultures where babies sleep snuggled close to mothers? Too many questions on this score for any single diary day. What if child is breast-fed—what! What! What!

Read about score of male undergrads accused of "lascivious carriage" with fourteen-year-old girl. Was she a Latin—from Puerto Rico? Fourteen is deep into adolescence. Why do papers have to run names and addresses at time of charge—before trial? And why is it "lascivious carriage?" I prefer "bawdy brougham" or "obscene auto."

Note in *New Scientist* that catamarans are in use on the Volga—250 feet long and 50 feet wide. The single hull with its historic beauty is on the way out—just as the adz has gone into history.

Last night a mixed party at 2 Fifth. Dave and Helen Loth [38] to report on his visits to Vatican, British Museum, libraries, to look into treatment of so-called Pornography. Of course the Vatican has no such attitude as exists in London or New York City—"Pornography for Scholars Only." Lena Levine came in at nine and Maggie warmed up a meal for her. Mag [39] came over and it was good to have her. Then Winnie, our Nantucket cook of last summer, brought me a box of her wonderful *Schnechen,* and stayed to chat. We didn't solve all the problems of our universe, and this group knew that if we could solve them, they wouldn't stay solved.

Roger H. over during the day and we will work up a plan to make the ceremony of citizenship as dignified and beautiful as admission to any private fraternity—or B'nai B'rith or Knights of Columbus. Incidentally, Howard C.,[40] an estimable citizen, a recent Catholic convert, was, according to the Press, given a high church decoration for "contribution made to the R. C. Church while U. S. High Commissioner at the Brussels Fair." What price joinder of State and Church? The Church should be more circumspect.

[38] Author and wife.
[39] Sister, Magdalen Stetten.
[40] Howard Cullman.

Thursday, January 28

A song sparrow arrived from North America to England. Some engine in those wings. Our jet is nothing compared to it. This is better than the warbler that flew from Montreal to Liverpool in 1955, for it used the deck of the S. S. Saxonia, and the sparrow may have traveled on its own power.

Two high spots. Thirty-five years ago a clerk in Schulte's secondhand book store—one Pesky—was arrested for selling a copy of Schnitzler's *Reigen*. He was convicted—Judge Lehman, a lusty male, voting for acquittal; Judge Cardozo, a celibate, voting for conviction. Sentence suspended. I had filed briefs in the Court of Appeals. Thirty years ago I applied for a presidential pardon for Pesky and got it. I recall I was outraged that a clerk should be convicted when the publisher was allowed to roam with immunity—untouched. I did the chore not for money but for greater satisfactions than cash. Today I'm told by Margaret that the Quinn letters in the libraries are typed copies and that the originals were sold by Quinn or his estate to Pesky or his company. So—bread does float on waters for decades if not cast there for purposes of rewards. Wilfred Pesky, the son, tells me he will dig up all records he has to help me in behalf of Farrell and the case against the library, which wants a distorted paraphrased market place rather than the accuracies and truth that come from copying the Q. letters. I feel elated.

The other items: I saw at Lester Cowan's request, his picture on the adoption of a Nazi youth in 1946 and the difficulty of re-education of the lad—with the symbol of reformation being so simple and true—the kid had never cried. Tears were the evidence of his return to the human race from the darkness of Hitler. This picture on which I'm consulted can be an instrument of diplomacy, for good or bad, and I hope that

L. C. takes my advice and gets Adenauer to clutch it to his bosom, introduce it to the German movie audience, and thus undercut his antisocial advice of desperation, "Beat up the people who put swastikas on churches." The movie serves love instead of hate, persuading the mind rather than subduing by fists.

Friday, January 29

Long day. Early plane loaded with Plimpton [41] and other Amherst alumni trustees to Washington. So I start the day in a Williams minority. The day ended at a party of Nixon supporters—Finch, Mundt, F. Lewis and others. I had just left the Humphrey headquarters at the Roosevelt Hotel and enjoyed, I must say, the friendly needling which the Nixonites always give me. Tried out on William White and Karl Mundt my idea that the Republicans were trying to change our form of government to a dynasty, with the vice president to become by tradition the automatically next elected president—this the result of stopping all contests before political conventions.

In Washington heard some of Stanton's [42] testimony at FCC. He's in a box, and I'm sorry for him. His logic runs: Government should keep hands off content of programs; applications for licenses should be chosen on the basis only of engineering, skill and honor (he knows no slide rule to test honor); the applicant's proposals for public interest should be supplied, and such promises shall not be looked into except as to his efforts to *find* societal needs; on renewal the Commission should not look into the successful applicant's promises

[41] Francis T. P. Plimpton, lawyer, later Ambassador at U.N.
[42] Frank Stanton of C.B.S.

for programming because by so doing the government would have to appraise programs. Q.E.D.: status quo and anyone who gets a license has it forever—even for sale, without any control by the government, except to examine "honor" of purchaser. So Stanton is smoked out—he believes man can correct himself without outside controls other than his own private appraisals of public comment. Is there no philosopher-statesman to speak up for the networks?

Lunch with devoted State Department officials who sadly say: Don't try to have the Department do anything brave or adventurous during an Election Year. This has always, they say, been the year for defensive plays only. So even if mass media for literacy were the only way to save Cuba, we must wait until 1961. Sad because with Ike in office they may be right.

Saturday, January 30

To office for gay talk with Patric Farrell and a gay lady friend, scholar and teacher of sixteenth-century English literature; lunch with zippy, restless Helen Buttenweiser, recent convert to sailing and—typical of her glands—rushed into the tense competitions of sail and wind. Swapped our worries of today's violations of due process and flirted around my buying her 36-foot yawl, now that she has a Pilot.

Home for reading; ten minute nap; talk with responsible Steffie who came for the night—always a pleasure.

Then to dinner at Rickey's with Mike, Connie and André Deutsch.[43] Too much trade gossip—typical of lawyers and other professionals. Cass [44] is one of the few publishers who does not easily slide into: "Who got Smith's book"; "What

[43] British publisher.
[44] Cass Canfield of Harper's.

did A pay for the Timbuctoo rights?" Then the Styrons [44a] came to the table and I stayed with them for a coffee. She's beautiful in my eyes, and he has much ideational space to travel before he will even know where he has to or will travel. But he will surely travel and go to places he will define for himself.

Sunday, January 31

One hundred twenty days or a few less and we'll be in Nantucket—back to our beach and work bench and boat. Read papers and again cut out highly conflicting headlines in *Times* and *Tribune* on our recent government report on Cuba.

Read Ed Williams' [45] manuscript again. It can be great but lawyers should never start to make a point by statement of theory, but always by reciting facts before the court, and then going into decisions reached. The reader must ever be part of an *ad hoc* audience vis-à-vis every expert of every profession. Experts find that vernacular of each profession is an obstacle to communication.

Mail comes in—my *New Leader* letter and with one good point: Those who believe (or enjoy talking as if they believed) the Atom Bomb would destroy all of mankind cannot lead man. Good—man should not follow men of despair. Pessimists are Homo Duplex—three-fourths dust and one-fourth spirit. Their theme—the glass is never half full but always half empty.

To Chinatown for New Year's parade. What provincials we are in Manhattan to miss this great parade of a people who carry their culture with pride even though their children

[44a] William Styron, novelist, and wife.
[45] Edward Bennett Williams.

35

are called Roger and Gwendolyn. What a place for social scientists—why no delinquency, why did Tong warfare of my youth disappear, is the ghetto by choice or by economic barriers?

A wondrous present from Maggie. A set of shelves in our tiny bathroom for my soap, razor and shaving stuff. No longer do I migrate those two steps from sink to bureau and back in the mornings. Why did we not think of this long ago? If it were on a boat I would have done the job the day after purchase.

Today I was a New Yorker—I couldn't, or rather made an obviously inadequate attempt to, repair an electrical fixture. On Nantucket I would have relished the chore. Here I'm not in the houseboy helpful rhythm.

February

Monday, February 1

Delicious tidbit. I have just learned that a rich Texan owns an unlisted telephone company. Probably he and his thousand friends have a company with separate switchboard, and each one has a private book of numbers. Which reminds me that in a decade or so there will be no more telephone poles or wires, since all messages will go over the air. Good for beauty and bad for copper wire companies. Every good must carry a bad. Is there any more a benefit without an offset? So radio, it was predicted, would hurt the piano business, and TV would wreck the record business—of course none of this proved to be true.

To ACLU [46] for lunch—big good meeting and a pie for

[46] American Civil Liberties Union.

Pat Malin's tenth year on the job as our director. But as the Union grows in dollars and members, the Board leaves more and more to the branches. Seldom do we hear the call to arms of the old days—Who will go to Herren on the massacre case? Who will enter the arena against Frank Hague, Boss of Jersey City? Maybe our fights are of a different texture—a texture of education and policy statement. But there is no "maybe" in my heart and glands, for I enjoy most the contact with the opposing forces. So of course I could not sit on the bench as a judge; and hence treasure most, of all F. D. R.'s letters to me, the one in which he wrote, "You are a man after my own heart," because I told him I did not want an appointment to the federal bench. And what a lousy judge I would have made—and F. D. R. admitted *he* couldn't be a judge either.

Tuesday, February 2

A pot potpourri—as life so often becomes. Last night home, and there were Connie, Kathie and Nick; begged Nick to come overnight sometime. Met a vital downtown lawyer, McNiff, with a big law shop and still interested in censorship and people and minds; read poem of Mae Goodman in *Herald Tribune*—she's one of my writing relatives; saw picture of automobile thief and he looks like my father—a shock because I haven't thought of my father for many a moon; read that an English robin landed in U.S.A. (and a few days ago I noted that a U.S. bird arrived on British shores) so we have a birdie Fulbright or, as Maggie said, a Flybright; noted that the Gulf Stream has been warming up since 1880—page Benjamin Franklin who first discovered it; sewed a button on my pants to M.'s amusement, and partly to see her make believe she was disgraced for failing to do her wifely duties; recalled that as a kid I sewed a bureau scarf and was pretty good at scalloping and overlaid strawberries made on double rings of wood; women married between 20 and 45 years of age live longer than single ones. I note "married" includes widows and divorcees—is the ceremony a factor, or is there more likely some relation to a full sex life, whether married or not? Hurrah! Three new national forests have been created by presidential decree—of course this affects the lives of millions of citizens and hence is not worthy of important comment in our daily press.

To lunch at Wings Club with James Warburg whom I respect, often differ with, and profoundly envy. Envy because he is his own one-man pamphleteering foundation. How I would love to be so endowed.

New idea for me. The people with 1,000 calories a day must be run by those with 3,000 per day. And those with 5,000 calories a day, in lush cultures like ours, are also run by the 3,000 group. Is this a new prestige formula for health officials to use to prevent overweight?

To Connie's with Margaret to baby sit. Saw Aly [47] on TV. The program had much dignity for a medium and a culture that does not understand that one man can both play hard and work hard.

Wednesday, February 3

More conflicts of reporting on which TV might well comment. *Herald Tribune* says this A.M., "Temperature Range for Today—20 to 38," and *Times* says, "Temperature range for today—18 to 32. "That's O.K. for readers of both of our morning papers but I'd like to know the source of each item. I'll bet it's the same Weather Bureau release.

[47] The late Prince Aly Khan.

At home with Sheffields [48] and Schwartzes to kid around with the Kavanagh Library fracas. Kavanagh was sued for publishing excerpts from Quinn collection of famous letters which he, K., had memorized in the library. We prepared a document for sheer fun.

Random Notes for Ladies

or

1916 Revisited

The following questions have arrived from Ireland hidden in the vest of a bedraggled member of the IRA who was imported for the ostensible but inaccurate purpose of posing for an Irish whisky ad in the *New Yorker*:

1. Who owns the right to publish the letters? Does the owner also retain the right to make a limited publication of the letters?
2. Assuming that the letters are of public interest how long should this interest be submerged under the cloak of private ownership?
3. In this connection should one who wants to reveal the contents of letters to the public be required to trace the heirs of Dante, Washington, Grover Cleveland, etc.?
4. Which law of ownership is to govern a letter written by Dante, the law at the time the letter was written or the present law?
5. To what extent does the theory of fair use permit one to publish excerpts from a collection of letters which have previously been the subject of a limited publication?
6. Assuming there is a right of exhibition in the receiver of letters, is this right transferred with ownership in the originals, or is it transferred with the ownership of copies of the originals? Does not the exhibition of copies diminish the value of the originals?

[48] Frederick Sheffield, attorney for N. Y. Public Library, and wife.

7. Is not the exhibition of letters by a quasi-public institution a dedication to the public?

8. Are not restrictions imposed by such a quasi-public institution upon the dissemination of knowledge in violation of the First and Fourteenth Amendments?

9. To what effect are policies and laws of foreign governments as to those letters written outside the United States?

10. What effect is to be given to a provision in the will of the original recipient of the letters providing that two volumes should be published for general circulation?

11. How extensive is the practice of limited publication by libraries? What kind of material is thus withheld from dissemination to the public?

12. How does this suppression of material affect our government in relation to papers affecting its activities? Should a distinction be made between governmental license and historical license?

13. What literature is available on this whole field of "secret documents"?

14. Is there a fixed common law rule as to the length of time such documents can be withheld? Would it be socially desirable to have such a rule? If so, what should the rule be?

15. How does the rule of limited publication affect the work of scholars? Is it not more socially desirable for history to be accurate rather than garbled? Should society be forced to rely upon vague recollections of historians as to the nature of original documents or should we not have our scholars and historians quote accurately from the original sources?

16. Would it not be helpful to have the opinion of a number of scholars on this subject?

17. Is there not an analogy between the "dead-hand" restrictions which create limited publications and the "dead-hand" volition of testators? If public policy can curb the latter why not also the former?

18. Assuming we were able to create public policy with reference to letters such as these and were not bound by dead-hand restrictions what rule would libraries consider most beneficial

to society? What would be the value of a foundation or "royal commission" study of this problem and their recommendations?

19. Have we not reached a point in our civilization where we can establish a clear and reasonable standard for the dissemination of knowledge which is derived from a thoughtful appraisal of the needs of our society?

20. How can these questions, and the many others which relate to them, be intelligently and comprehensively resolved in the context of the present proceedings?

21. What Irish whisky do you like best and why?

Thursday, February 4

Great pleasure last night. This is the way to practice law when issues affect our nation. The Sheffields were delightful and I mean literally "full of light." How easily controversies can be resolved if there be a smitch of good will. The method of the future to induce gifts to libraries, plus the widest possible diffusion by the libraries, may be ripe for solution. I'd enjoy watching the mind of Archie MacLeish applied to the problem. He's a lawyer and writer and was Librarian of Congress. So we are on our way, and as a bit of velvet Freddy S. told amusing tales that were handed down to him by his father about Garfield, Churchill and Teddy R.

Note of cheer—not of course in press—518,000 Negroes have been integrated in the schools—one-fifth of total. Far to go with the other four-fifths, but a first page story showing we are on our way would accelerate the balance of the march from here on.

To dinner for Japanese food which I have a passion for every few months.

Friday, February 5

Read about a toy store operator in Philadelphia who has invented 30 different games for the blind—which he and his family produce in a garage to give to hospitals, schools and homes for the aged.

Last night saw Vinton Freedley,[49] Radie Harris [50] and Ilka Chase at a showing of *The Race For Space* at the 67th Street Armory. Audience full of generals. It's a great movie on the origin of rockets and the missile race. Disturbing proof of the lethargy at the White House and the excessive worship of budget balancing at present tax rates. We need a president who talks in terms of "sweat and tears"—for our people would love a leader who calls for dedication and sacrifice. The picture came into focus when Mike Wallace, the narrator, held an order in his hand issued to all Defense personnel—an order in the form of an iron curtain—"No official should mention space or missiles." The general in charge of later questions, Major General Toftoy, could not tell when it was issued or who wrote it. But surely any president who permits such secrecy by mandate has no doubt issued last week similar decrees of darkness. And this was no secrecy in military terms —properly withheld from people by the rulers. This was a taboo of an entire area of subject matter. Want to have ACLU show the picture to a special audience.

Wrote a letter to Will Yolen [51] who sent me a Gillette razor.

I write at the moment about some further ideas I have with respect to the relation of old-fashioned razors to the capacity of the mind of man to make a leap. As I explained to you, Churchill got his best ideas, he once said, while in a hot bath with a big

---

[49] Active and important in the theater.
[50] Writer about movies, TV, theater.
[51] Public relations expert.

cigar and a glass of scotch. In our culture which is in truth a rat-race life, man only gets a good idea when relaxed, and this is usually under the following circumstances: falling asleep, waking up, taking a hot bath or shaving in the morning. I have long argued that Ed Murrow was our best commentator because he had a thick beard and it took him a half hour to shave every morning. His competitors shaved in twelve minutes, so Ed had a head start of 18 minutes, to dream and think and invent. To be sure, those who are rushing through life saving minutes which they waste on all kinds of useless projects will find at times that the electric razor answers their purposes, but I rather think that the leaders of society are those who realize that man never gets a good idea while busy or while waiting for a half dozen telephone calls. He gets a good idea while loafing in an automobile, in a sailboat, on a beach or, best of all, while shaving every morning. As to women, they get their best ideas while sitting at a beauty parlor for two or three hours with nothing to do but dream and ponder.

My previous letter and this one may together give you a lead for a wholly new adventure of an amusing type—to distinguish your razor from the electric razor just as the shower bath can be distinguished from the tub. Of course my name is not to be mentioned under any circumstances but if you wish to talk to me further to develop these random ideas, don't hesitate to get in touch with me as I have given years of thought, while shaving, to this very thought.

Lunch with intelligent record-maker—Arthur Klein. I'll bet on his purpose, motive and integrity. Our society has only started to use records as a culture medium, although Caedmon has made a glorious dent and a start on the problem.

Saturday, February 6

On the way to the office I carried on with a bit of day-dreaming that started while at my fruit and coffee in bed. Which of my friends at the office has lost the ability to cry with tears? And I mean crying alone and not public moisture, for the latter is of a different quality—not for oneself but for the audience.

The cleric takes on a cloak of humility because that to which he looks up has been personified—a man on canvas—Confucius, Moses, or Jesus or Buddha—while we lawyers cast upward an eye toward that impersonal image, The Law. Even the witch doctors personified the witches with whom they dealt. The soberness of the law is that we who practice at it want to meet standards we each create for ourselves, and, if we get near our own goals, winning or losing takes second place. People uncertain of their own standards must pay undue regard to victories. As Bennett Cerf said on television, he who has no standards shows up as a ham person. B. C. didn't quite say this to himself or aloud or, to put it more kindly, didn't know he said it.

Fulton Lewis wrote a column on me and a chat I had with him at Irving Ferman's [52] home. He's an odd duck. We saw eye to eye on so much thirty years ago at Drew's [53] parties. I reproached him for what I deem his errors with a smile and good will. Compared to Sokolsky and others of the so-called Right he is the smartest and most accurate. So I'll get thirty letters from friends calling me a fascist; I go to Colombia for Monsignor Salcedo and the mail says, "are you becoming a Catholic?" And when I represent a Communist against the government, I'm branded a Communist. So what!

[52] Washington lawyer, now high official of International Latex.
[53] Drew Pearson, the columnist.

45

The Williams Mirage: Sunday through Tuesday, February 7, 8 and 9

The last week end is a merged parcel, containing a variety of nonfungible bits.

Friday started it all. I was getting ready for my Williams experiment. Many pleasures came my way, I'm sure, but now on Wednesday, early, lying in bed after breakfast, I recall first and hence most clearly that we had a few hours of sentimental music: "The Wayward Wind," *Show Boat,* DeBussy, and best of all, Kurt Weil's *Lost in the Stars*—the piece which I lived on when sick in the hospital just as others stay alive on blood transfusions. The heart is fed by more than blood.

Saturday was a nothing in retrospect—all blacked out by acts I didn't want to do or acts I don't dare recall. But Sunday starts the crescendo of "Billville."

Drove to Williamstown in Irving's car past the signs marked "Deer crossing"; complaints at inadequate road signs—no distances indicated; missed out because of lousy oil company maps the turn-off to Cam Beckett's—that wise barrister who left a giant law shop on Wall Street to practice in civilized fashion in Lakeville; tense driving in Berkshire snow flurries; finally Williams Inn.

Then I spent the best thirty-six hours I have spent at my college since the September morning when as a solitary lad in 1905 I first arrived there. For dinner with Professors Clark and Rhoads, specialists on foreign aid and education. They are deep in the new venture of a college for foreign students —graduate types from less-developed lands. Discussed how they will select the twenty, what happens to them after the year's work, limitation of students to English speakers, and so forth. Good talk until long past their bedtime.

Monday A.M. to library to see an exhibit of 1776 to 1787

documents—remarkable and worthy of riding circuit to all other colleges. Then to book store—posing as Dr. Gallup—asked every customer: How many books have you read this week, this year—just for pleasure, with no relation to the burden of reading prescribed by professors. Answer was generally speaking, "None except during vacation." Then lunch with the Iconoclasts—the upperclassmen who are not in fraternities. Talked about hypocrisy of chapel attendance—or any mandate to become spiritual or religious. Suggested that an inquiry be directed to alumni to find effects, and to trustees to discuss their "worshipping" patterns, if any, after leaving college. Too bad the college treats the undergraduates as adolescents—with many regulations and few chances to learn from man's best instructor, Responsibility, and from the opportunity to make one's own errors and pay one's own penalties. To a lecture at an economics course of Clark's; a seminar on socialism; discussion on effects of cost accounting reminded me of talk with commissar in Moscow. How are consumer choices decided if there be no profit system—between hair do's or picture post cards or five inch TV sets? Who decides what new lines of consumer choice to invest government money in? Then to talk at Professor Connelly's group of forty prelaw lads. Surely they haven't the least idea why law might suit them. Made clear I was a bad advisor—anti-ABA type—have had too much fun and luck at the bar for fifty years, have forgotten most of the trials and tribulations of the early days.

Then to dinner with Dean Brooks, retired Professor Newhall, Professors Burns and Connelly. Why should faculty be kept in a dither of darkness as to next prexy of college? Are scholars unfit to pick the boss of scholars?

Then to Talkathon at Jessup Hall. Not too successful. Two to three hundred in audience. Spoke on Population Explosion, and then questions led to Curse of Bigness of corporations, unions and governments; censorship; TV quiz show problems and probably thirty other topics. Did well on some and flunked others. After one and a half hours—say about 9:30—I had a station break. About one hundred walked out and I explained that was O.K. and that I'd quit when bored but must believe that the men and women of quality were those who stuck it out. Went on until about 10 P.M. and then to Commons with a group of about fifteen or twenty until about midnight.

Learned much about technique of colloquy to replace lecture. I enjoyed it and imagine many in audience did also after getting over the surprise of entering a hall and not hearing a formal lecture. One thing is sure—informality is destroyed if talker is not on same physical floor-level as audience. At Jessup I was five feet higher on a platform. That negates equality.

Tuesday drove down to city—much irritation with roads, car, ice; to office by 2 P.M.; to Mag's for dinner with top biochemists, Hans [54] and friend; home really pooped out—which rarely happens.

More brain food in Williams in two days than New York City in a week.

Wednesday, February 10

I failed to mention a significant item in my week-end comment. There was much snow—clean snow, pure snow; and the heavens for at least a day and a half were Maggie's shade of unvarnished, unspotted blue. It was cold but a clean dry kind of low temperature. No wonder I felt so elated and happy.

[54] Dr. DeWitt Stetten, Jr. of National Institutes of Health, nephew.

A kindly letter from Dickie Ernst [55] who wrote that he spent a week end with me—meaning that he read the Atheneum version of *Touch Wood*. He and Maggie Cousins are my first fans—other than my own Maggie, prejudiced by a long love.

A stream of letters and interviews from people who think they have grievances. Most are off balance, few have even a pretense of a sound legal position but—this is the damnable part of my use of time—I can't refrain from reviewing each one, for what if by chance one screwball happens to have a good legal grievance? Law is not a mass of statistics or even averages or mediums—it's uniquely personal for each and every human being.

At New York University Law School for presentation of the Jerome Frank Awards to police who have done distinguished service for civil liberty. The winners were fetched from New Orleans; the honorable mention awards went to two New York City detectives. No TV station was interested in a broadcast. If one of the nonwinners had shot one of the judges—God what a story and a headline! But the gathering was spiritual. The N.O. police chief came along and reported that the Mayor of N.O. had given medals to the persons we were honoring, and Commissioner Kennedy of New York City mounted the platform too and then and there—as a surprise— promoted, one grade each, the two recipients of our awards. They were surprised, telephoned their wives who thought they were kidding and, as one suggested, had already spent the $800 increased salary. Edmund Cahn [56] spoke well of Jerry,[57] and Irving Younger of Si's [58] office ran the show with dignity. New York University did a meager job of public relations, but I have no complaint—didn't the faculty of Yale Law School refuse to accept the Judge Jerome Frank Fund

[55] Richard Ernst, relative and financier.
[56] Lawyer, teacher, author.
[57] Judge Jerome Frank, former partner.
[58] Judge Simon Rifkind.

for the awards? I spoke about some of Jerry's dreams and passions, of his hatred of the press, and TV interviews of persons just after arrest and before being booked at the station house. Kennedy arose in part to make answer to me since I suggested an arrested person stands on hallowed ground—the Due Process Spot—where no one should talk to him until he has a lawyer and has been informed he is as immune as if in a cell. The police should protect him and advise him not to talk; anything he says might be held against him. I learn that the wire service gave the lead, "Kennedy and Ernst in an argument." Filthy. Me they can't hurt, but Kennedy may not like it. I'll not even correct the press, on an old theory—don't ever get into a pissing match with a skunk. Kennedy can't go far for due process because the press and TV misconstruing Freedom of the Press will chew him up.

Home for dinner—all at ease and in peace.

Thursday, February 11

To Overseas Press Club for meeting of Magazine Writers Guild. About forty persons. Once more I watched young, eager people play with the intricacies of the democratic process. A new plan for nominating and electing officers— a plan which unwittingly was an attempt to compromise between continuity and fresh blood, between youth and old age, between stability and opposition—all reminding me of the thirty-nine gentlemen at secret sessions in Philadelphia in 1787, drawing up the constitution of the United States. Heard the stultifying report on what editors of magazines were in the market to buy. Not a single good idea, for it concedes absence of originality in the writing and validates the word "hack" ("hack" from "hackney," a horse let out to hire—

hence "hack" means "worn out," "commonplace"). The buyers say in effect: If you hack this out we will buy. Whether the writers care or not is quite remote from the report.

Then to Bessies' where Maggie was baby-sitting. Bessies and friends came in after theater, and we watched the Jack Paar show—with Paar walking off stage. It was good drama even though the liberals will say "but he is a difficult guy, he is a so-and-so," overlooking the point that only the off-beat arouses society to do battle against complacency—the Brouns walking out of the *New York World* on the Sacco-Vanzetti issue; the Kavanaghs and Farrells waking up the Library. So Paar does battle. I was glad I telegraphed him in the afternoon before I knew that he was going to reject N.B.C. censorship without a hearing. Even Adam and Eve got a hearing *before* being thrown out of the Garden of Eden. I wired:

JACK PAAR

I know nothing of the merits of your controversy but I am delighted about the public debate because wisdom only grows out of argument and not out of assertion stop The network if it had wisdom would welcome the debate relying on the wisdom of the American people to find truth in the matching of wits in the marketplace of thought.

Cordially
MORRIS L. ERNST

To bed at about 2 A.M. It was a thrilling episode. What if Sarnoff had appeared on the show and shown the piece censored, stating bravely the authority of N.B.C., but saying men of good taste may differ, and because Paar had had no hearing the public should decide.

Friday, February 12

Received some Valentines. Always a pleasure and I never guess from whom. But the first says, "I'm Yours," so I go to every attractive girl in the office, show it to her and say, "Thanks very much."

Joan over before I went to office and reports of the new baby cat which Steffie calls "Boots."

Dictated outline of piece on Juvenile Delinquency and my plan for approach through prize fighters and airplane hostesses—the hero and heroine of the leader and his moll—symbols of prestige to take the place of void vacated by parents, teacher, policeman and cleric.

Neat idea. In the unasked-for clutter of subsidized second class mail I receive daily about eight or ten self-addressed envelopes. I think I'll send them back with nothing in them or with some unasked for other advertisements received that day. If such a move became popular the entire racket might come to an end. Mentioned this to Penelope and she says someone at the *Times* had made this proposal in a different form. She also whispered that England has plans for a trans-ocean boat that will go from London to New York in two days; about 3,000 tons, she says, and carry 1,000 passengers —cabins like good trains, semihydrofoil. Boy—we are just starting!

Home—loafing, reading. We need no things and Maggie does the shopping and marketing without a peep to anyone so that it all seems effortless. But at Williams the wives told us when the men do the marketing the bills are higher, the luxuries more prevalent and the time spent greater. Page Paul Revere and all the men until about the turn of the century when we first allowed women to go marketing. Historically simple, I guess. We males took our products to market (Revere his silverware) and then bartered for other produce or sold and bought. How come in Burma women run the shops—what status that gives them!

Sunday, February 14

Quite a few Valentines and could not even spot Maggie's.

To office for several hours to dictate letters to Carrie's [59] cousins to give her a book of poems, letters or cartoons for her eighty-third birthday. Then to movie, *Sapphire*, with Maggie and to dinner at Voisin with Margalo,[60] who is my most gallant friend.

New York Times has an editorial captioned, "Mikoyan's Cuban Coup." Sad. "Coup" carries an element of suddenness and surprise and I guess Herbert Matthews of the *Times* was taken off his feet, never wanting to believe that Cuba was to be the first economic base of Russia in the western hemisphere. Who can open the eyes of Matthews—or rather his glands?

After writing this I picked up the *Times* of Monday, February 15, and my desire is satisfied. Reston says the Communist infiltration has gone so far that it may not be in the power of Castro to control it. And last night Mrs. R.,[61] Muñoz,[62] Rockefeller and the editor of the Christian Science Monitor were on TV on Cuba, and it was sad for it was no doubt taped before the Mikoyan visit. N.R. showed up best— he had done his homework. Muñoz, wise as ever—a truly great person.

59 The late Mrs. Jerome Hanauer.
60 Margalo Gillmore, actress.
61 Eleanor Roosevelt.
62 Muñoz Marín, Governor of Puerto Rico.

Cold winds. The family temperature gap is important—more than the missile gap. All young couples should be temperatured before marriage. A small gap is good—as a base for give and take—on weight of quilts, windows open at night. But if the gap is too big there are many problems—for example, the big double bed is out.

One nice memory. At Voisin for dinner, crowded room and one of the captains across the room saw me, and instead of nodding as if I were a customer, he waved a hand as if I were a friend.

Tuesday, February 16

Breakfast with director of WBAI, a new nonprofit experiment in radio. No sponsors and support voluntary from public, $12 a year minimum. It can service our people until many other stations adopt the same system or until we have Pay TV in which event WBAI will be able to make an easy and comfortable shift-over. Must listen to the station—which is at a handicap until the 50 million captive audience, automobile-radio-set listeners are equipped with FM. May do a weekly program for WBAI but am still concerned by its implied involvement with communists—undisclosed. A disclosed communist is a good communist because we can lick him; the concealed one is a danger and a bit of indecent humanity.

Lunch with Dick Ernst at Overseas Press Club. I enjoy his agility of thought. When he said he has given up reading hard science I realized that this attitude is accepted by many nonexperts. So I'll needle his mind by sending him the Science News Letter—a science fun magazine for adults of our generation and for kids of the next one.

At home a mob of under-thirties, men and women, with

wings still spread and chins jutting out and ears not pinned back, with problems and ambitions, hopes and dreams—all types from lawyer to teacher.

Wednesday, February 17

Last night's "two generations removed" party was awkward. I asked each one: "Do you want a grant to go anywhere, do anything?" Answers were blown up with doubts—giving no evidence of gnawing dreams. And I have so many —too many according to my friends.

Thursday, February 18

Although I got to sleep at 2 A.M. this morning, I was a purrer. Incidentally, why do cats purr—is it inspiratory and expiratory as with the donkey's hee haw? I understand it's only true with domesticated cats. Finches, I am told, purr for protection. But cats do not purr, I'm sure, as a protective instrument or as a means of communication. I'm like a cat—purr from relaxation, and as a reflex without conscious intent. And maybe spinsters enjoy cats not only because they represent sexual enjoyment but also because they, like people, express relaxation by sounds. And so—why don't I like cats on my lap or even near me?

To R. L. for an hour to get his slant on the function of a committee of the Bar Association to appraise the qualifications of a prospective judge. I'm in a quandary. Which of two values do I hold highest, the right of confrontation or the desire to get better judges—assuming that we can get better judges if at the same time conclusions are arrived at by using faceless informers? I start with a lifetime prejudice—to favor the right of each individual rather than to attain a better world by a rule which disregards any single human being.

But R. L. worried me with his insight into the overformalization of process of decision. I'm inclined to believe that I'll not have anything to say at the Bar Association meeting of March 2 about judicial approvals. I have listed up a score of questions unsolved in my mind. Everyone else appears to have all the answers. Lucky folk.

To Julie and Paul [63] for drinks. Good crowd. Particularly happy to see Frank Graham [64] and chat a moment about Kashmir on which he is still working. Then in real rain gale to movie which Joan recommended—*The 400 Blows*. Amusing that Joan should be wise enough to pick this picture of a pleasant nonblamable delinquent's life and misfortunes as being of interest to my tender spots.

Home and cooked our own meal. As good or better even than my favorite Voisin.

Saturday, February 20

Plane with Norman Poser to Washington. I enjoyed the sensations of introducer—taking a young open-eyed lad down an academy lane which he had heard about but never strayed in. The Hubert Humphrey braintrust picked us up at the airport and then for hours of coffee-drinking at the University Club. How will Hubert disturb and answer the Everything-is-O.K. Ike pattern—trust Uncle Ike, for he is not a father symbol (no sternness of eye or firmness of chin) but more like the kindly Uncle who says don't cry, here's a lollipop.

[63] Paul Herzog, American Arbitration Society, and his wife, director of Woodrow Wilson Foundation.
[64] U.N. official.

Interesting words exploring the difference between Needs and Wants.

I became excited about Phil Stern, whom I had followed at Democratic Party Headquarters, when he edited the meager Democratic Digest. Tried Dodd, Monroney and others—all off speech making.

Then to Irv Ferman—meeting NAACP lawyer. Why did not our own media let us know that a new building for Howard University (Negro) was built and not a Negro allowed on the job? Just a minor little rule of Building Trades Unions in the District of Columbia.

So home and to dinner with Judge Martin Frank and his judiciary friends. Enjoyed meeting again Judge Bonaparte who recalled an argument in the Court of Appeals when he was a district attorney—a modest magazine case. I had forgotten every detail. So I said, "You remembered in depth; I forgot it all. You must have won, and I forgot because I lost." And so it was.

Monday, February 22

What better celebration of Washington than the announcement from Harvard Hospital, Salisbury, England, that they have tested 6,000 people after ten days in isolation and will isolate and identify the virus of the Common Cold. Maybe we will find a virus like influenza that bobs up in odd years. We are at verge therefore of growing the virus and making a vaccine. I read it all but, of course, being an uneducated creature, could not understand the relation to the kidney cells or why the Common Cold is so touchy about the nose. But I still will keep my eye on the Heel—Hoof and Mouth diseases and relationships are not to be forgotten. Wet feet— and colds; swollen heels and inflated tonsils. But the C. C.

is a great enemy of man in higher civilizations. What of Russia —has it reached that level, now that it is getting to suicide and ulcers through personal frustrations?

So maybe in a year we will lick the moth and rust, the other great human household threats.

Tuesday, February 23

Well-paced day. Solitude but not loneliness. Law and life merged in fairly decent fashion. We shall celebrate our start at 2 Rector Street, under the Elevated Railroad, in May, 1915 —four of us, equal partners, and one employee, Ethel Hirshman, who was bookkeeper, office boy, stenographer and telephone operator at $15 a week—which was the amount of our unguaranteed drawings if, as and when clients paid fees sufficient to pay for rent, telephone, Ethel, stationery, etc.

So I asked the file clerk to get me out the first dozen files to look at the causes, the clients and what we did to spend our time.

It's evil to have backward eyes, but a squint into the past is a satisfying sport for the fortunate man. Although he may be a bit wiser, history—even personal history—can point to errors to be corrected under similar conditions in the future. Only man can employ that boosting technique. No mouse learns that a trap is associated with cheese. Only a Pavlovian man can train—not educate—a dog to repeat a joy or avoid a misery. Our biggest asset is unique—it's history.

Wednesday, February 24

Erich Remarque in office and admiring my furniture. Why not beauty in my office, where I spend more time than in any room at home except the living room in Nantucket? Affectionate letter from Rust, Editor of Esquire, on *Touch Wood*. I made an offer for a 36-foot well-found yawl. I hesitated a long while, but why should I wait until I'm seventy-five or eighty to buy my last dream boat? Nicky to office. He enjoys the Thermofax, the adding machine and, above all, dictating for twenty minutes to my recording machine, hearing his own voice and putting on a show as if he were a newscaster on TV or radio. What would he have done before TV? I gave him a piece of marble from Hitler's library at Berchtesgaden—given to me by Leonard Lyons in 1946.

Dinner at home—too many people but great fun with Cass, the Vogts,[65] Leona and Nat,[66] Mary C.[67] We solved population problems—but they won't stay solved overnight.

Called Bob Lovett [68] to thank him for his wisdom at Senate Committee hearing. Wise, thoughtful and nonpersonal. True our Republic is doing less well than it should. We need a leader—but there is nothing a new president can't cure.

Sent my Joyce-inscribed copy of *Ulysses* to Chicago for appraisal by Ralph Newman.[69]

Thursday, February 25

After dinner, Alan and Paula came in with Alan's mother and father, and then for some odd reason which Maggie and I could not explain, we acted like very ancient old folk. We started to reminisce. Interestingly enough what poured out of me and Maggie were a great number of stories dealing with Carlo Tresca. We told how Carlo, the head of the anar-

[65] William Vogt, population expert.
[66] Dr. Leona Baumgartner, N.Y.C. Health Commission, and her husband Nat Elias.
[67] Dr. Mary Calderone, planned parenthood specialist.
[68] Robert Lovett, banker, government official.
[69] Literary appraiser, Lincolniana.

chist movement of our nation, had been thrown out of Italy when he was working with Mussolini, at that time a leftist; and then we told one story after another. This frightening anarchist used to come to our house for dinner and always brought a rum cake or something soft and sweet for us and the kids. Carlo had a long love affair with Elizabeth Gurley Flynn, and when it was over Elizabeth, whom I had known quite well, left the IWW and the philosophical left and became an active and devout Communist, even going to jail for that quixotic, cowardly and sneaky group. I recalled how Carlo had gone to jail for printing a two-line advertisement of a birth control book; and how through the intervention of the Secretary of State, Charles Evans Hughes, a deal could have been made to drop the indictment if Carlo had been willing to go back to Italy, which would have meant execution. I told how Carlo had collected a lot of money in Sacco-Vanzetti case and then was held up on the lower East side of New York; and, in order to get the money back, he found a very simple device. He let it be known to the underworld that this money was clean, nice money—it wasn't robbery money. The very next day, through the underworld, the robbers were located, and the money was returned to Carlo. Story after story came back. After Carlo left Atlanta Penitentiary, where he was sent for the birth control advertisement, he had a few hours stopover in Washington and went to see the White House. Outside a group of school children were assembled to be shown through. Carlo, who looked like a doctor with a beard, was carrying a black bag. A child was hurt, and thinking Carlo was a doctor, they asked him to aid. The next thing he knew he was with the school children on a tour of the White House. He and I had a good laugh when we pondered what would have happened if any detective safeguarding the life of our president had located Carlo, the anarchist, just out of Atlanta jail. Carlo wouldn't step on an

60

ant. I mentioned something that happened while Carlo was being shaved in jail. The barber, also an inmate, recognized a knife wound on Carlo's face, and suddenly said, "I know you, I'm the person that made the scar." Carlo was always broke, and many a time Maggie and I helped to get out his issue of Martello, the "Hammer," when he needed $50 or $70. He always called it a loan and never thought of repaying because he really didn't believe in debt or any kind of honor that related to property. But he was a peaceful soul. Once when the fascists were following him around New York, he got a gun, and one day when he thought he was being followed, to scare off the person who was trailing him, he fired through the pocket of his coat—and as inevitably had to happen to a leading anarchist, he shot himself in the leg.

Maybe I should do a book of small profiles dealing with the people I have run into, such as Tresca; Roger Baldwin, the capitalist anarchist; Louis Brandeis, the economist jurist; Heywood Broun; Texas Guinan, union leader; Russell Leffingwell, the man of wisdom; John L. Lewis, man of culture and toughness; Harold Ickes, the man of many jobs; Genevieve Taggart; James Joyce; Fiorello La Guardia; Mary Ware Dennett and others. I had engaging and entrancing relationships with all of them and have piled up in the back of my mind hundreds of amusing gay stories dealing with their eccentricities—they are all eccentrics in our culture, except possibly my friend Russell.

Saturday and Sunday, February 27 and 28

To lunch at Voisin with Paul DeWitt [70] and young lawyer to talk over the big rowdy meeting which takes place on March 2 at the Bar Association. I suggested that the issues

[70] Officer of the Association of the Bar of the City of New York.

should be stated so that men of good will might differ. On the one hand the right of confrontation for the judge who is up for appraisal; on the other, the need of supporting blindly the Judiciary Committee which frowned on this judge. But in historic terms the cowardice of bench and bar prevents the right of confrontation. Men are afraid to be other than faceless informers—so we shall probably never even be told the names of the committee members who voted for the judge, and those against and those not voting.

Dislike taking a walk—enjoy a stroll. But Sunday I was browbeaten into a walk by author-jurist Martin Frank—he with a beret, and me a coward afraid to wear mine in front of a judge. Good talk, ending up at Bessies' whom he enjoyed.

Isn't it true that old people look at their watches less often than youngsters? At least that's true with me, as it should be. Even though I have probably only 4,000 evenings left, and should hoard minutes, I don't find that I do so.

Great Hockey game—U.S. *vs.* Soviets—3 to 2. Particularly enjoyable because our Rangers of New York have been so miserable that we have deserted Reed [71] and his Garden. Likewise the track meets have become meager—last Saturday the new high jump champion did not even show up.

Weather good—a little white coat of snow on the grass parts of the Square.

A week end of great quantities of kidding between us— giggles, silly jokes, puns and those memorable minor key instruments of communication between people who have shared the same bed and board for years and years.

[71] The late John Reed Kilpatrick, Chairman of Madison Square Garden.

Monday, February 29

Early Maggie and I went to see Bergman who is working on globes showing height of land and absence of water. Much work has been done by Russia on such data—with maps from Norway, beautiful and exactly three-dimensional. I bought a 12-inch globe showing mountains in some exactitude—but there is no globe yet showing our planet without water. What a globe that will be—with the line of present water levels. Thrilling time—although the clash between scientists and merchandizers is as ever disturbing and requires a Dave Sarnoff who can act as governor or arbiter between these two powerful forces—the salesman versus the scholar-scientist.

Great sun in the sky and temperature and much joy because Steffie's teacher told Maggie about that kid. A visiting teacher sat in the class and asked about that well-adjusted child—and then was told her parents were deaf. How come? they all say. As do we.

March

Tuesday, March 1

Our Wedding Anniversary—the 37th—all good and rich.

My diary for the day is short and sweet. It would burst at the seams if I added anything more as prelude or an afterlude. On my bureau, with a bottle of coffee brandy, I found the following from Maggie:

Translation of a Latin poem by Ausonius:

My husband, let us go on living as we have lived; and let us keep the names we gave each other when first we went to bed together. And as we change together in time let no day ever bring it that I am not a young woman to you still and you a boy to me. We are to be the sort of people who won't know what full old age is like. The thing to do is not to count up what your age is but to know its quality.

Wednesday, March 2

Many enjoyable meetings yesterday. Drew in town and Maggie and I alternated talk with him at lunch with Jackson Lighter. Drew looks younger than a decade ago. He has so many exciting facts—for example, we gave Ecuador enough wealth in jet planes so that we could have supplied an entire educational system instead—schools and all for that little country.

Saw Anatol Shub, formerly of *New Leader*. Cultured, rounded editor. He has an idea for a new magazine—pick-up-translations in the main of articles on all levels of cultural interest from foreign lands. Does not interest me, and I explained to him what I want is a pick-up magazine popularizing new knowledge in the minds and writing of scholars, down to my possible understanding. Syndicator of 8,000 weeklies came to chat about a new plan for servicing those important outlets with vital new material—plus a convention of the editors whom I am asked to address.

In the evening I threw a party for the entertainment committee of the Bar Association—the group that had needled me when I was selected as the Twelfth Night Leading Lawyer Goat of the year. It was a great party—and I felt (with Maggie out) like a prospective bridegroom throwing his bachelor dinner. I was an adult male with no trace of insecurity in front of these big-shot barristers, including two delightful judges. After all had gone the bell rang at midnight and another lawyer, Sherman, and wife came in. They found me half undressed, and felt ill at ease thinking that the party would still be going on. They stayed and we talked of Nantucket which they also love.

Chatted and kidded, bed to bed, after lights were out for an hour or so. Far better than sleep.

Thursday, March 3

Reading "The Bystander," a novel by Guerard, reminds me that I was first in love when I was eight or nine years old. In the dining room of a summer hotel I saw a lady sitting alone at a table and could not take my eyes off her. Of course I don't recall her looks—they have been montaged with hundreds of female faces. But I guess she was buxom and brunette, and I'm fairly sure that I tied an apple in ribbon and left it sheepishly at her place. Or is this all a bit of make-believe from a story I heard or read. Anyway, I'd like to meet her now. This is the Guerard theme—and I enjoy it.

At the bar meeting last night I was ashamed of the caliber of debate, the lack of dignity and the absence of any real feeling except for one speech on the values of fair process—right of confrontation, bill of particulars and the like. An inquiry by the Mayor (to cover him up) resulting in disapproval by a committee—twelve for, four against and one not voting. And no one asked the twelve or four to stand up and be counted. Some price bravery! And the condemned judge never faced his informers, his defense did him no good, and the addresses were not up to debates I have heard at the Newspaper Guild. I would have put in my two cents except I had talked to the Ruling Team at the Bar Association and felt squeamish about then attacking the process. But I voted against the motion because it approved the procedure of faceless informers—a procedure which will decrease rather than increase bravery among lawyers.

Saturday, March 5

At office and read agreeable letters from Frank Graham of U.N., Rundquist of Senator Clark's office in Washington; learned of Hiram's [72] fixing of end of September for publication of *Touch Wood;* visited with Detroit couple of West-of-Hudson attitudes; lunch with Bill Astor [73] in from London, and so it went.

One letter makes me think of kinds of people and kinds of woes. I suspect there are three types. First are the worries borne by men and women and assuaged by reporting them to dozens of friends or even strangers. These vary from a cut finger to missing a train. They are seldom significant but comfort comes from relating the facts—often in boring detail—to deaf ears. The second category consists of what man deems mighty and profound. So these woes are taken only to one, two or three people. The real woes are those which some people learn to carry all alone—because telling does no good, because telling only worries the rare selected receptacle, and, above all, because the sufferer must be his own doctor, priest, lawyer.

My troublesome clients are in the second category. They are poor souls who try to live isolated, remote lives, believing that people can live in these terms—one by one. These are the most difficult cases but also the most gratifying; although on them and on the spreading types I try to impress the importance of not talking to anyone else while talking to me or the doctor or the divine. This works if I'm acute enough to get to the client's mind. If not, she wanders into every stupid alley trying to get confirmation of her prejudice and to prove that my advice is not for the best.

[72] Hiram Haydn, partner, Atheneum Publishers.
[73] Viscount Astor.

Sunday, March 6

Sleepy day what with window-gazing on the Square and reading. Carl Rode has written a delicious bit of history, the story of our culture from 1840 to 1861. I'd like such a volume every twenty years—including music, newspapers, painting, books, songs—a real dip into the changing moods of our people. To me it's more exciting than the anthropology of a Pacific island. What a destiny we clasped to our hearts until the past decade destroyed our assurance and optimism. Then read halfway through Bob Heilbroner's *The Future As History*. It is a dire attempt to be hopeful; but his conclusions, I'm sure, will show that we are a defeated rather than an optimistic people.

Delighted at reference to Maggie's book *In A Word*—with Thurber pictures—in Saturday Review. Went with doubts to Phoenix Theater to see Henry IV. A great show, good fun, and only wish I could have seen it not knowing the name of the playwright. I do feel that it's so full of wise lines that I could not grasp them all at once—the great flood of ideas requires a second take. And surely the audience of Shakespeare's England was not only the elite but included bums and vagabonds—the itinerant players of that day were such. So what did the audience understand and appreciate? Was it spoken at a much slower pace? Or did they comprehend faster and better than we today?

Tuesday, March 8

A rushed day—no good for legal invention. In the early morning talked to thirteen-year-olds at City and Country School—where I first took Connie about thirty-six years ago,

Roger later, and where Maggie ran the library for seventeen years, and now Nick and Steff are in attendance. Discussed 1787, the Founding Fathers, the Constitution, the courts. A bright, informed group. Started with a tough question: How did Hamilton, a delegate, get to the Philadelphia Convention from New York City? Answer surprised them all. Sailboat at Murray Street Wharf (three days a week—wind permitting) to New Brunswick, coach next day to Trenton and third day coach to Philadelphia. $3.25 with blankets on Mercereau's Flying Machine. Good fun was had by me and I hope by them.

To office and spent five hours with Otto Vega [74] who wanted ideas on three Dominican Republic programs: survey of liberty—which I turned into survey of police and courts; comparative study of twenty-five-year progress in health, education, industry and agriculture—which is useless unless made in comparison to other South American nations; and techniques toward political freedom and a two-party system. I suggested the need of starting in villages and on issues, rather than with people or candidates, and then outlined the Ayub Khan Pakistan plan of democracy in villages until people can communicate and read sufficiently for national expressions of desires. The sterner the dictator, the more I'm intrigued, and the more the necessity of gradual steps toward freedom.

To New York City ACLU dinner at Commodore. Tom Henning [75] direct and simple as usual, but all affairs and dinners are a goddamn bore. This will be my only public dinner for 1960.

[74] Official of Dominican Republic.
[75] U. S. Senator.

Wednesday, March 9

In the morning to Pakistan House with Minister of Finance and Economic Minister of the Pakistan Embassy in Washington. Discussed the great wealth under the ground in that nation. These people are brilliant of mind and brief in words. A relief after spending time with Irish or Latins.

Then to Downtown Association with Eddie, George Roberts and Bill Chanler of the Stimson office. Sound barristers and engaging people. What happens to these types when they run the Bar Association? Why in a group are they so unimaginative? I worried them by asking what they have done with the Elihu Root file of the last century. Of course, as expected, it's all in a warehouse eating up money. All of it—subject to client confidences—should be in a public library and taken as a gift in tax deductible form by George or the Root heirs or someone.

To see the Thurber show. What an antic mind has Jim. Subtle, cerebral and full of ingenuity as shown in production by Buzz Meredith. Ran into the Thurbers, Nugents and Jules Goldstone at "21" after theater and we closed up the joint at 2:30 A.M. What a guy Jim is—making believe he doesn't enjoy the great success of his show. Many of the skits derived out of incidents we lived through with him. So we recalled the past. Most of our then pals are dead—Benchley, Broun, Mencken, Nathan. But Jim is alive and argued that hearing improves when ears are used for the purpose of being pinned back, and chins are employed to be stuck out to be battered.

Thursday, March 10

Interesting lunch with Barry Cohen and happy he is happy with his own shingle hung high as Counselor at Law. Discussed my affirmative plan for a proper, nonfraudulent function of Vanity Publishers in our society. Thousands of men and women scribble and can't properly get a publisher. Most of the words are not worthy of the trees wasted for paper. But the urge is a good one, and many will pay to get their "opi" in print—for their friends and their egos. Thus the business comes in on fraudulent terms, promising editions and distributions never hoped for by the so-called publisher. We worked out a plan to cut out misrepresentation. Too bad in our culture the attack is so much more delightful than the solution. On this issue the publisher groups and the government—more particularly the Federal Trade Commission—have done only the accusatory part of the job. Once more people say: It was good that Hercules cleaned out the Augean Stables—but no one said he had a duty to fill up the stables anew. I prefer to let others rake the muck if I am allowed to come up with the next forward steps.

Weather great. Clean sky, crisp temperature. The streets are covered with dirt on top of mounds of snow, a sight impossible in Nantucket.

Goldies' [76] for dinner—delight.

Friday, March 11

My saddest day of 1960. Years ago I endorsed a note for $1,200 for a social friend of our home. The payments were not met. I paid up. The $1,200 was a sizable sum but not out

[76] Goldstein family collectively.

of line with the affection I bore the friend. But I lost the friend—lost irretrievably. His shame created the chasm. He was silly to believe that the money was so important to me. I liked him more than I did the $1,200. But this he could not believe—so I never saw him again even though I wrote and begged his forgiveness.

And today the person outside of close friends and family on whom I have showered most benefits, and even wealth, took a similar attitude. The shame of not being able to balance the books led not only to walking on the other side of the street to avoid my glance but even adopting an attitude of undermining me. I guess I'll never learn that it is much easier to give than to receive. Few people can be benefactees with comfort and ease. Terribly hurt. Maybe because I guessed wrong—once more—on character of my former friend.

Trev Gardner for dinner. Fine mind, alert attitudes and enjoyable guest. No wonder he left the Ike team—which is scared and unadventurous.

Saturday and Sunday, March 12 and 13

Gay weather and hot sun.

Most important. Maggie woke up at 2:35 A.M.—the very time of the eclipse of the moon. Out of a deep sleep she got up and saw the moon in its covers. Why did her unconscious remember to wake her up? And why did she let me sleep and thus, as I accused her, "hog the eclipse"?

Sunday to the Roller Derby at the Armory on 14th Street. A different audience than at any other sport. Poorer folk, more vocal and with more enjoyment of sadism. Nicky enjoyed it.

Saw "Open End" on TV and enjoyed sober conversation between Catholics, Jews and Protestants about Birth Control and Church and School conflicts. Senator Eugene McCarthy shone—in fact outshone the Rabbi and Bishop Pike. Great stuff of good will.

Too busy and excited to write more details of my busy life. But one item of science:

In Bengal, the folk living in the Lushai Hills died like rats validating the old legend—when the bamboos flower, the land is stricken. And so it happened. For the rats ate the seeds, and then ate the produce of the land as the legend said: "Like rats they will die with the rats." Folklore is terrific in its validity, and governments in India or the United States pay too little attention to Old Wives' Tales. Incidentally, there are no Old Men's Tales. The wives had time to think— an ingredient of intuition.

Monday, March 14

Four professors at Harwell, England, on January 30 verified Einstein's theory, or so it is headlined in *New Scientist*. What do we do—have a ticker tape parade up Broadway to match the recent one for Carol Heiss, the Olympic fancy-skating champion? And why do we not honor men of the mind as we do warriors and athletes? Once more I'll try to get our President to invite an educator or a poet to a White House dinner as F. D. R. used to do. Must we give White House prestige only to operators and politicians?

Tuesday, March 15

Letters from Connie in Paris, Mike in London and Jean [77] in Delhi. It's good they are all living fully—but we miss them.

[77] Jean Ernst, wife of son Roger, in India with Agency for International Development.

Carrie H. called up with tears in her throat to thank us for corralling letters from all of her cousins to wish her a rich eighty-third birthday. It made a handsome volume. What else can one give a dear woman who has all possessions money can buy and her heart can want. Carrie said she cried most of the day as she read the score of letters. But we know there are happy tears as well as sad ones. And as I left the phone I wiped my eyes for she had touched me.

Last night we went to the only great show in New York City. Hoffa of the Teamsters had a rally at Madison Square Garden. Up we traipsed not having been to such a rally for years. Recalled the Nazi, Communist, Socialist rallies of old. Reid Kilpatrick and I went to many a rally, to see the techniques of the enemy. Tonight there was little of the grand spectacle—Hoffa spoke for an hour and a half as a sober lawyer would have done, and held attention as no leader does except John L. It was well-prepared, not read, logical and not at all demogogic. The attack was mainly on Bob Kennedy and rather well deserved I do believe. He forgot he was a lawyer and acted as if someone elected him to our Senate. It was unfair to John Kennedy; bitter on McClellan but big applause came when he attacked the press, radio and TV. Not as frightening as I expected—but it would be well to have early discussions of the danger of excessive power of unions that move merchandise. We can get along without any one commodity, but the truckers control all commodities. I'm not much concerned with the corruption charges because law cannot readily regulate honesty in networks, or unions or corporations—although no corporation would want to repeal the Security Exchange Act. Left meeting with no emotions. It will take me a few days to appraise Hoffa's appeal.

New York *Post* has a good ad in the *Times*—a list of a dozen top Eisenhower employees who have been asked to get out of government because of lack of ethics. Not deep freezers but real payola of the most concealed and subtle varieties.

Wednesday, March 16

I never thought I would read that in the park in Havana people are shouting, "Kill Ike."

Last night hied out to see the latest Bergman movie *Lesson in Love*. Great, sensitive producer with the same Swedish cast. My mind jumps to difficulties of our speech with its sloppy use of words—"In love," "making love," "love," "loving" —all get confused in our literature and in the imagery of our movies, TV and theater, although they are quite different emotions and behavior patterns.

Many "lovely" bits of a home today. After my shower knelt down by Maggie's bed, brought her scissors we bought in Toledo—those with the inlaid engraved gold handles—and Maggie clipped the hair around my ears. I don't want two clusters of hair like Ben Gurion—but I dislike going to barber shops.

Other item. A girl of thirty-five or so, with wedding ring, falls asleep opposite me on the bus. Query: Should I wake her up, or should I let her pass her stop. Trouble either way—so being an essential coward I wake her up by what she will think is an inadvertent brush of my foot to bump her.

Brought in breakfast trays—an odd size—and Maggie reminds me they were bought to fit the dumbwaiter in our house on 11th Street more than thirty-five years ago. Good to live with things for decades. They become part of us.

Up to office early having dictated to Nellie, my home machine, so P.G.[78] says to one of the lads, "He needs no sleep." I say, "like Edison, but he produced light and I create

[78] Paula Gross, secretary of a lifetime.

darkness." And what's wrong with that? No good ideas come under the bright klieg lights or even the sun when it is directly overhead. I'll spread mellow darkness—the climate for leaping and strolling minds, as well as the time for making love, being in love, feeling lovely and live the forty or fifty concepts of love for which the Greeks had separate words.

To lunch at the great library—42nd Street and 5th Avenue —with the Chief Librarian. What a wonderful atmosphere to live in. As with most of my hours and conversations my pen is broken and my lips are sealed. T'ain't mine to utter. This is one of the limitations of working in a profession. Those damn clients own my communication system.

Thursday, March 17

St. Patrick's Day—must avoid the parade. Stayed at home with my dictet. Then to Hiram to discuss new books I have in outline. G. W. & E. luncheon at Williams Club. Ran into Potty Whittemore, Williams 1907. Potty has been his name for sixty-three years. Why, I ask? When eleven years old he had a big belly—probably, he says, he ate too many apples. So his name is Potty. Mine at college was Dutchy. An Ernst of German origin graduated the year I entered, and I inherited his nickname. It's useful at times. People meet me and if they say, "Hi Dutch," my mind must dig into my Williams brain file. Dean Kirchwey, of Columbia Law School, went to Sing Sing Prison as Warden late in life. He once told me if he met men who said "Hello Dean" he concluded the person had been an inmate at prison, and if the salutation was "Hello Warden" he was sure it was a student from Columbia. And now Maggie is called Marguerite or Sammy only by her Wellesley pals. Others say Margaret.

Goldies at home for dinner.

Friday, March 18

Conference with an important ex-Admiral of our Navy. I'm humble before admirals—more so than before generals. Does this derive from love of sailing which gives me humility toward Triton and respect for the tops of the Navy?

Letter from Teddy Z.: [79]

DEAR MORRIS:

In view of the fact that you are one of the few people I know who appreciates the charm of being over 70, I thought I would pass on to you a remark of one of my colleagues, who has just passed his 76th birthday and who observed that he has now been in the public domain for 20 years and is advising your ladies that he now can be used without charge.

I answered:

MY DEAR TEDDY:

I loved you at fifty and the hunk you have of me has never been in public domain. In truth, I am in your debt.

Switchboard out of order at office. Wonderful. I announced I had ordered a score of quill pens, postal cards to replace calls. What a relief it would be. I told people that at the Constitutional Convention in Philadelphia in 1787 there were no loud-speakers, no typewriters—only James Madison who wrote out in longhand every word of the four months of debate (wrote it twice—no carbon paper invented at that time). He wrote it all except when he spoke on a few rare occasions. Madison was not the Secretary of the Convention —just its main architect.

[79] Theodora Zavin, lawyer at B.M.I.

Saturday, March 19 and Sunday, March 20

Not too gay a period of life. Can't put my finger on the reason. Weather favorable—all well except Maggie's slow-healing wrist—Nick had a bad night. So I list events—at least a few. At office, a lad who wins prizes in words and numbers wants to talk about going to Williams—On my Joy Meter I hit 47; my best-informed friend on Caribbean drops in to tell me latest news of Panama (41); lunch with Mrs. Kermit Roosevelt, a good R, Democrat, gallant inquiring person (64); an hour with Tillie Losch who moved from dance to painting and now to nonrepresentational art (62); reread *A Modern Symposium*, G. Lowes Dickinson (78); reread *Abramson's Mind* and *Death of a Genius* (85); looked at a few questions in galleys of *Touch Wood* (−75); saw Benny on TV for five minutes (−10 for each minute); read *New York Times* Book Reviews while in hot tub (92 but count 32 for setting of tub); South American news in papers more depressing than ever (−60); plea for more patience re Cuba sounds like Munich of Chamberlain's day (knocks me down 300 or 400 points); Ad for Book on Useless Knowledge—will send in coupon and $1.00 (94); heard Maggie's travel dream with Katharine White and Mark Van Doren—fantastic (worth at least 100); gay letter from Roger Baldwin who cheers me mightily and says, "I know you'll continue to operate a one-man lifesaving station for those who come to you." (70); letter from Bob Fowler [80] with a good quota on international aid (37).

Maggie interrupts to remind me that our son Roger and I used to rate girls (he was 20 and I was 55) from one to ten—standards undefined but agreed upon. Years before that we

[80] Montreal Newsprint Association.

rated our friends one to ten on Sanity. Dotty Parker claimed 11 for herself in those days, and when we gave Rollin Kirby the cartoonist a rating of 1 he threatened to sue for libel—who wants to be sane (dull). Maggie also suggests at this point—noon on Sunday—that she wants to see the weighted totals at end of the day.

Saw my ear operation on Charlie Collingwood's TV show —and then to Ellen D.—beautiful person—good food—much recall of Nelson who befriended me all of his life.

Home early and to bed reading Ferber's revised *Peculiar Treasure*.

Monday, March 21

Lunch at O.P.C. with Robert L. Heilbroner whose new book is important and may seep down from the top of our culture. He and I differ only because he does not share my hope that leaders will arise in our government, unions, businesses and foundations to make us face up to the conflict between the speed of relief to the underdeveloped lands by communist dictatorship, as compared to the sturdy, slower democratic techniques for increasing productivity and reduction of population. I tried to sell him my optimism by explaining dozens of little, tiny techniques available to us without vast benefactions. I think he agrees, except he feels our land lacks the affirmative and the spiritual leadership. And I should not let him out of my reach.

Maggie has her hands overflowing. Joan's maid is ill, no baby sitter available, Nicholas is sick—and so Maggie rides circuit.

Tuesday, March 22

Breakfast at Aly Khan's. I enjoy him greatly, partly because his background and life are so remote from any experience I have ever lived and partly because he is so simple and direct.

Rog writes a lovely item from India. Why are the people of Kerala so tidy and clean compared to the balance of India and the East? Answer: great amount of Christian influence— which means folk go to church which demands fairly neat dress for worship. Thus the Hindus who worship at home have no standard of dressing clean at least once a week.

Nantucket is agog. Big democratic debate—hearings, letters to press. Three hundred people are for a new bowling alley—many against. The existence of an alley is of minor importance. Man can live without a bowling ball; but the democratic process is significant and at work.

Also *Town Crier* has a deserved and tender editorial note on the contribution of Jane Lamb on the school board, and a word of cheer for her in her defeat for re-election. In New York City no one knows the name of any member of our school board—or where it meets.

I'm an author. Pat Knopf gave me a dinner party with book critic Tinkle of Dallas *News* and others. So I'm no longer a scab writer. I'm in the profession at last. Good food and gay talk. No reforming of our globe.

Wednesday, March 23

Troubled by New York State allowing New York City banks to take over the state. The easy road to statism without the need of communists. Presidents of small banks will be put into Gargantuan grinder and come out as robot clerks. When will the big boys learn that man must be allowed his own chances to make error if he is to grow?

Rampage that lawyers for indigent people who are hit by autos are charging too much. Without factual base 50 per cent seems to some to be exorbitant. I wonder if the negligence bar gets rich? I'll bet I could reduce the service in half by an inquiry into the insurance companies and their outrageous delaying habits and tactics.

Saw in press Pegler is getting a divorce. Will this spell out a bit of mellow in his acid nature?

To lunch with Judge Irving Kaufman and some of his confreres to discuss his provocative article in the Atlantic Monthly. Then chatted with Circuit Court judges and was kidded that I wrote too many books. Defended by saying, "But after a book is in print I have often changed my mind." To which Learned Hand says, "I have difficulty in changing my mind." "Surely," I replied, "because even though you do not claim infallibility, you are too often right." He replies, "That's not the reason. Rather I'm not sure enough as to what I believe."

To Book Award party at Astor. The symbol has become meager and no longer carries either great prestige or increased sales.

Thursday, March 24

Had fun writing many letters. Here's one to Jim Bennett about the problems that arise at time of sentences of people found guilty. There are no standards, great variety depending on the judge's appetite, sadism and sensitivity. Hence this letter which I enjoyed thinking into words:

MY DEAR JIM:

I assume you have seen Judge Irving R. Kaufman's article which appeared in the January issue of *The Atlantic Monthly*. I was sufficiently intrigued to waste a few minutes of the Judge's time. I have just had lunch with him and some of his confreres. I have only one tiny idea that may point to a new approach.

We have had a deluge of knowledge on the subject about which he wrote. For my part, in most spheres of the law I think our shortcoming is not the absence of facts but the inability to operate on the knowledge that is in our possession at any moment of history. Surely with respect to the many questions he raises we should not wait for unanimity for if there be unanimity there is no need for action since life takes care of the unanimous. I suggest that what we need is a new prestigeful leadership and I make several points on this score.

In the first place the leaders of the bar, or more precisely the leaders of bar associations have disqualified themselves since such eminent lawyers have neither concern, interest or knowledge in criminal jurisprudence except for two polite crimes—those of wealthy income tax evaders and anti-trust violators.

In the second place, bar associations operate through committees, and committees negate the possibility of action. A committee is a process designed by man to reach a pleasant compromise at the lowest common denominator, with the result that no member has any sense of urgency in his belly sufficient to carry on.

In the third place, lawyers, particularly the leaders, perform the valiant function to society of rendering an opinion and advising some ulcerous vice-president of a corporation how to carry on. Hence, the library shelves are full of dignified knowledge assembled by lawyers, which volumes are little more than secret autobiographies. Lawyers are not operators either for themselves or their clients except pushing money across tables or as advocates in a court room.

With the above in mind, I suggest that our society must find a new prestigeful symbol equipped for leadership for action. Maybe nothing should be done until the Circuit Conferences have wended their weary ways and have pumped out thousands of words in thoughtful but impotent resolutions. The thought came to me that it might not waste too much of your time if sometime when you are in New York, you and Irving and I could have dinner together. I will supply the wine or other lubricant needed for maintenance of good will.

Am I merely a dream boy to think that our Chief Justice might designate a master and accept financing from some Foundation? The master should not be a research type. He should carry enough impatience to see something happen before he dies. He might assemble the knowledge *now* possessed by man in the fields discussed so acutely by you, Irving and others. His function might well be little more than making specific recommendations—(a) for the spread of existing knowledge; and (b) for action by judicial rule, legislative enactment or otherwise.

For my part I would always rather have one man write a book than a committee make a report, and a master reporting to our highest court might be listened to sufficiently to arouse all of us to action. What the master would propose of necessity would not meet unanimous acceptance. Hence, the need for a new symbol of leadership.

We don't want anybody to write another book or report which would do no more than give the author immortality for a short time. All that I wish you is a tiny hunk of the same even though you may think this letter to be fruitless.

P.S. The judges I sat with acted just like lawyers and no more. Each went off on his own tangent on a specific reform and none would keep his mind on the objectives I uttered, namely: invent avenues toward action.

On Barry Gray's radio show at 11 P.M. for an hour. Always enjoyable—although I don't know why. I guess I'm a suppressed editor or commentator.

Friday, March 25

I told some of the youngsters in the office that I had been tagged Director Emeritus of the ACLU. I said "ex" means "without," so the total means "without merit." Mary Wenig came back at me with the following: "emeritus" from Latin *emereri*—to earn one's own discharge. Literally to "earn out."

Newman Levy [81] drops in after Frank Adams' funeral. Frank did more than Woolcott, Broun and Benchley combined, for while he left no writings of enduring value, thousands of young men and women wrote for his "Conning Tower," and F. P. A. created standards which innumerable poets, critics and writers were eagerly trying to reach. He was an important teacher in the best sense.

To theater to see Tony Perkins' play "Greenwillow" and then to Sardi's for dinner with Ferber and Joe Ream where Tony met us later. Gay.

Saturday, March 26 and Sunday, March 27

Last night "Greenwillow" was my kind of musical. Joe Ream agreed—Margaret and Edna dissenting in various degrees. And I'm glad Tony joined us at Sardi's later—a delightful, outgoing person—at least all that goes out flows with grace and without hindrance. I'm interested in what doesn't flow or show.

Figures come out in expensive study by American-Marietta Company for 1975 population and output of U.S.A. Delighted, for people laughed in 1955 when I predicted a trillion GNP in my Utopia 1976. Now the estimate for one year less is about 925 billion; and this lower figure is derived from

[81] Lawyer, author.

an estimated population of about 235 million or 15 million more than my guess.

Just learned R. L. off to hospital. Worried. Where? What? Must try to reach his close friends—but all out of town.

Lovely Helen Reid [82] for lunch. New York City's greatest woman citizen. Must get her soon with Aly and talk about the Near East. People like Helen and Aly are quiet in their diplomacies and so can be effective.

A new island erupted off Ecuador—and it is 125 feet above sea level in no time at all.

Planned Parent Bulletin most heartwarming—all kinds of wholesome attitudes toward religious rights and duties of Protestants, and amenabilities of more and more Catholics.

Sunday, Bonis [83] gathered architects, librarians, lawyers, critics and authors for breakfast at Enrico and Paglieri, and Alan and I discussed the Farrell-Library matter. Everyone there had an answer except Dolbier [84] of *H. T.*—but soon all understood the need of rethinking the entire problem of letters given to libraries and right of family to control publication.

Judge and Mrs. Martin Frank dropped down for coffee after dinner.

My day off—with little if any energy. Tired blood be damned. It was tired mind for me all week end.

Monday, March 28

R. L. at St. Luke's Hospital, not serious except that he's no youngster—even older than I am. He's on my mind because he holds a separate niche—an irreplaceable one.

[82] Former owner of *Herald Tribune*.
[83] Mr. and Mrs. Albert Boni of Readex Corporation.
[84] Maurice Dolbier, book critic.

Spring weather. It may cheer me up. I've been low—mainly out of worry about what is happening to the United States of America. Our people are not overwhelmingly in the Need Class—but have the Want Class habits corrupted us? Are we individual isolationists, each worrying only about himself, and buying absolution by donations of money for charity for those in need? Are we unconcerned because our mass media keep us uninformed? Are we complacent because TV and press place main emphasis on the evil—the destruction of life's events? Everyone cares a little about everything, but too few care a lot about something. We need a leader with fire in his belly.

Tuesday, March 29

Hours of mental tournaments with various clients. So many want affirmation of their desires rather than advice.

The big time was with a social scientist who brings me projections for Argentina and Bolivia in comparison to the U.S.A. in the year 2000 as to gross national output and per capita income. It's worse than I thought. Our head start is our burden. The gap will increase. Only under dictatorships by a tight control of a society's mobility can the production be increased. By swapping Freedom for things, the masses under government controls can keep up with population increases. Even a 7 per cent per annum increase of production makes the world look sad by the year 2000. Of our GNP, only 20 per cent is used cooperatively by government—elsewhere it runs as high as 80 per cent. With the Soviet it is nearly 100 per cent. So some suggest that we would be better off if the communists took over all the backward nations, had the headaches, and earned the envy and jealousy which is now directed at us.

R. L. came through the operation in top shape. Considerate of Harry Davison to telephone me. I telegraphed R. L.: "Hurrah, Hosannas and hearty thanks."

Read great article in *Harper's* on the future of the democratic process, particularly in illiterate areas trying to conceive of a two party political system. Even in our land we did not have or think of two parties in meaningful terms until 1812. The candidate with the second highest vote became V.P. So Adlai instead of Nixon under Ike. WOW!

Wednesday, March 30

What makes a day in total, in summation? I know no technique for over-all appraisal. I list a deluge of delights and still feel unsatisfied. Are my values changing? I wish I knew.

Today, for example, I heard that David Susskind may take my suggestion and do a TV show on literacy and the democratic process. I read Capote's gay *Breakfast at Tiffany's*. A letter comes from my friend, the Archbishop of Canterbury, on the subject of World Population. I dip into da Vinci's diaries—rare perception. I read Leonard Moore's thoughtful and disturbing 90-page-long opinion in the Lady Chatterley case; a big foundation lets me know it will subsidize me as a kind of one man foundation for jobs sorely needed in the legal areas. I'm invited to a meeting at a fighting paper that is ready to announce the solution to the Galindez mystery despite the embarrassment to our Government, *The New York Times* and *Life* magazine.

Why don't I preen myself on these and dozens of other minor or major satisfactions?

In another area, I'm tickled by the census-takers. I hear that one out of four or five of the citizens of our land are being asked forty or so questions about ice boxes, cars and the like—everything but important questions such as religious adherence, reading of books, attendance at art galleries. And Maggie and I naturally are not in the select group. In my 71½ years no one has ever polled me on any subject under the heavens from presidential choice to tooth paste. Poor Maggie—she's been tainted. She once was called up and asked her preference of candy bars—and I, with a giant sweet tooth, was passed by. I ain't even a statistic—I don't enter into any averages or medians. I'm just a solitary human— tabulated through others.

Sweet note from R. L.'s daughter about Russell, comfortable at St. Luke's.

Thursday, March 31

It's easy for me to admit error and change my mind, even after I have publicly declared my position. But to change a basic attitude or philosophy is a dish of a different taste. So now I'm upset—or at least one of my tenets is disturbed and wobbly. For half a century I have believed that political freedom rests on a two-party political system. One party equals dictatorship; many spell chaos. But now I am near to believing that illiterate, inarticulate folk are not able to choose between two candidates. The most they can do is vaguely to debate a simple issue—where to put a new well in a village. So the entrance to democracy may not touch political freedom in terms of parties. What worries me most is that I am forced to recall our own nation in 1787, when there were differences of opinion between Jefferson and Hamilton; when 250,000 people, out of a total population of four million, voted on the Constitution; when troops had to bring in delegates to attend the Convention in Pennsylvania in order to get a quorum; and, above all, when the issues were so diffused that the candidate with most votes was president, and the runner-up was V.P. How then does Pakistan or Dominican Republic have an election even in a city? Maybe a limited, elite electorate was the secret for our use of the franchise. Gradually we extended the right to vote. If all men and women had had the right to vote in 1791, it would have been an unintelligent mess. In the dictatorship nations, to start an opposition party would be impossible on account of fear; and impossible, because the result would not be believed and cynicism toward the ballot box would be the residue.

A thousand doubts and queries go into my mind just because I have taken for granted the simple fact of the right to vote and the handling of elections. Above all, what will be the issues even as to people—since in our land the differences between parties are vague, and as to candidates in a party, little more at time than popularity tests?

This damn problem spoiled my day. I wrote to friends and U.S. Ambassadors in dictatorship lands to read the article by Erskine Childers in *Harper's* magazine of this month. It jarred me terribly.

April

Friday, April 1

Walked into the office with a bad feigned limp. Everyone asked what's the matter. Answer: simple—April Fool's Day. This I do believe is a better technique than saying, "What's the hole in your dress?" Without words, the fooling is more acute.

Last night, while reading, Maggie and I coincided in observations. I say: Does the Freud ethic emphasize freedom to choose at the expense of choice? M. says: Does freedom lie in having a choice or in making a choice? The latter, I suggest.

From there I pick up from da Vinci or somewhere the fact that neurosis is the penalty of ambition unprepared for sacrifice. I like that, but I'm still in doubt because I do believe that neuroses are infectious. I know one gal who spreads her neuroses just as if she were Typhoid Mary. Contagious even. Or does this mean that she can infect only those whose ambitions are not geared to acceptance of any sacrifice? Or do some neurotics live on and off of suffering?

Lunch with Alan who sees law as I do—an outlet for creative urges. And what a field it is since most lawyers go little beyond craftsmanship—which is of supreme importance but not enough as an end-all.

For dinner at Lena Levine's—always engaging people and relaxed moods.

Saturday, April 2 and Sunday, April 3

Week-end rains made all of life a little dull. At office Saturday most of the day, save only for trip to Ken Heyman— friend of Hiram and suggested as a photographer of informalities. There met a young Negro lad who had been high in a city gang and cross-examined him as to power of the moll; monogamous folkways of leader of gang—but only as symbol of power. Who are heroes of gang leaders—prize fighters, criminals, jockeys? And of molls—WAVES, WAC'S, nurses, actresses or airplane hostesses?

In evening to Horner's [85] where an intelligent attractive woman of late forties, to end a difference of opinion, threw me a final epithet with churlish lip—"You idealist you." What does this spell—in an egg-head era, in days when hard science can dream, in days when poets have betrayed us by going anti-idealist?

Sunday, home with M.'s bad back all day except that I took Nick uptown to belly-laughing movies—Chaplin, Hal Roach, Arbuckle, Mac Sennett—all old silent films but funny beyond

[85] Harry Horner, theater designer.

anything of this era. In evening turned the TV knob to look at an advertised satire, a Jack Benny. I didn't get a single smile.

Missed Marie and Penelope, particularly the latter because of science reading and queries. Is it true that we know the ingredients of ocean water but can't make it in a laboratory? Why is desalinization so important, since on the average there are only 35 parts of salt in 1000? Since sound travels five times as fast in water as in air, why is not water the base of hearing aid? Hot water, cold water, coffee, salt water, whiskey—maybe some one of them is 50 times as fast. Why books called "Silent Oceans" and the like when the sea is so noisy, with the sensitive-eyed fish at certain levels and the blind ones at others? Is luminosity just a lure? I would have thought if we can see thirty yards in the water, fish would have adjusted to see further.

Read Sunday papers—which seem much like radio and TV. I guess da Vinci was correct. When words uttered or written contain no emotion or feeling the memory of man reacts negatively to the ideas. The press in its search for objectivity is in the mood of not caring. It is so unemotional that it is losing its desire even for fairness. The reporter knows the headline will color his article, will pick an attitude and will not want to attract readers by objective fairness. Maybe I enjoy the *H. T.* because its prejudices are publicly avowed— no concealment, no effort to be an unconcerned god of the printed word. Maggie suggests I go to London and hire Marie for a week's talk. I wish I could afford it.

Usual law day with its indescribable variety.

For dinner Gordon,[86] Laura [87] and the Schwartzes. We talked of madness of the theater as an economic unit in our society. I think it's the only business about which no one knows anything. The people who give their lives and money to it don't even know the size of the total audience or whether it goes up or down in any season. The corruption is high, wide and handsome. Estimates run as high as $10 million paid for tickets in excess of the box office prices and never returned to the theater for the actors, investors, directors, stage hands. Thus the real gross has little relation to economy of the theater. If the sum siphoned off on ticket prices went into the theater, the cost of productions could be carried so as to survive the unfavorable reviews of two or three top critics.

Laura much interested in the Sacco-Vanzetti case, and I gave her part of my story of talks with the leader of the gang that committed the robbery and murder for which S. and V. were electrocuted. She's some gal—representing all the dignity and good will of her great family.

Maggie's back is bad, but doctor dopes her up to reduce the pain. Yesterday a Communist youth convention took place in Havana—represented by delegates from Russia and U.S.A. —and little, if any, mention of this in our press or TV or radio. I can't figure out why. Is this an aftermath of McCarthyism— people afraid to be anti-Communist for fear of being identified with McCarthyism?

Note that an Arizona court held an antimiscegenation statute unconstitutional. Good. Why should we allow the State

[86] Gordon Rogoff, editor of *Theatre Arts Magazine*.
[87] Laura Rockefeller Case, friend of Paula Schwarz

to dictate patterns of marriage—save only for minimum age and bigamy? Both of these grounds may well concern the State because of absence of parental control, financial burdens on the state, or because of fraud.

Tuesday, April 5

Penelope will return soon from her deep-sea adventure. I miss her. She never laughs at my improbable questions about the ways of nature.

Note that nephritis may be related to tonsilitis. Tonsil swellings are truly a barometer—nothing in themselves, just outlets for other ailments, like a pain in the heel.

Diamonds, I read, are more than a girl's best friend; they may be the base of a new supersensitive thermometer.

Last night Tella [88] and Roseman [89] at the house. One of my best evenings—youth showed me its better side. They are willing to gamble their futures to do a research job and book on the growing gap in standards of living between us and the rest of the world. Surely the gap will grow between United States and India until 2035. So we will figure out, on the basis of population rates (fairly inflexible in the near future), what the rate of production will have to be for any backward people to start to catch up to us by the year 2000. We have jogged along for decades at an average 3 per cent increase in gross national product. Assume other lands hit 7 per cent or even 10 per cent—as China is reputed to be doing—when does the Envy Gap close up? Does a poor man only want to equal his rich neighbor or does he, when he equals his Envy Symbol, want to pass and go further? So the rich in India want to reach us and better us, and while they

[88] Economist.
[89] Demographer.

95

travel this path the gap within India increases—and for more internal envies. But envy is a driving force for betterment. Anyway we must get out a book on this disturbing thesis.

Maggie a little better.

Wednesday, April 6

Lunch with Ross of M.C.A. and Cantor, TV writer, to go over my TV Good News program. We may not get a sponsor because the idea is unique—based on an assumption that the audience does want words of hope and good cheer. I refuse to believe the contrary assumption of Madison Avenue that only bad news is news. In a one-inch story today in the greatest of our papers, the *Times,* my eye caught an item: a Negro Baptist minister runs for City Council in Slaton, Texas, defeats all five white opponents and is elected. Think what the story would have done on the front page to change the attitude of New Yorkers toward Texas. It might even be welcomed by thousands in other cities of Texas—where the press also runs only the saga of man's defeats.

For dinner at Williams Club meeting of Gargoyle. Main discussion involves admission of Negroes to fraternities. The undergraduates are a generation ahead of the president and the trustees. The colloquy was more disturbing than any talk I have had on techniques for integration of swimming pools in Texas. Maybe the college is worried about the unmentionable factor of house party troubles when white girls will meet a Negro on social terms for the first time. I'm glad the talks were not recorded for distribution in bigoted India.

Got page proof of 1958-9 *Touch Wood*; Steffie sent home from school with a fever; Maggie's back is irksome; ponder at Hiram's suggestion letting him get a writer to do a biography of my random life. Sent a draft of essay to Emory Law Review (it's a letter to a grandchild on the romance of the law); read *American Scholar*—enjoyed piece on Decline of Utopia by Kenneth Keniston; looked over Nieman Fellow *Reporter, Listener,* and a lot of miscellaneous semijunk.

Enjoyed article in *New Scientist* on characteristics of male asparagus and possibility of producing a species that gives birth only to males. Learned that the word Scientist was first used in 1840, "newly minted by William Whewell of Trinity College." Science Talent Institute announced that age of decision is thirteen, and 40 per cent of top students of science named teachers as most important in decision toward a life of science—25 per cent named a member of the family.

Friday, April 8

To Carnegie for lunch. Always enjoy these minds—remote from profit motives. This Foundation more than most knows that to fulfill its function there must be a high quota of failure and that the function of a Foundation is in part to take sober but brash gambles on men and projects in the search for reduction of society's pains.

A fantastic lady of the arts in the office told of her growing into professional adulthood—but remaining adolescent as a person. Beaux aplenty she has and will have. A rich great person—but no person for me to spend more than a few hours with at any one time. But one I far prefer to the steady, sober, bore types. Incidentally, she told of men who tell her they dream about her—to which she reacts by holding out her hand and saying $10 please.

Week End, April 9 and 10

It's top time. How the kids know it I can't remember—but there they are, the same small wooden differently-colored tops with metal pegs. Bright chippy days.

We can't even carry on a conversation, in a prepared forum discussion on TV, on any subject related to Homo sapiens. What a time Howard Smith had with top people on the question of leadership of mass media—from Leo Rosten and Gilbert Seldes who spoke as if they were so objective they didn't care; to Fred Friendly and Marguerite Higgins who had lots of knowledge but not enough to replace a "concern" with ivory tower objectivity; to Frank Pace who couldn't tell what he felt about leaders of government, business and press.

Great event of week. *Time* runs the payoff story on birth control—with Dr. Rock's picture—dignified and honorable giving Catholic position. This should be the turning point—other papers will reduce their fears. I would have thought that the *Times* would break the ice, but even the great New Jersey case was pushed in a corner by someone on the leading paper of our nation.

Several walks on Sunday—one to east 10th Street to see a short block with a dozen new art galleries. Slept much of the day on and off and felt not up to shaving; or didn't shave and thus felt less than on my toes.

Baby-sat at Goldies' Saturday evening with the cat making love to me to such an extent that we locked her in Joan's room.

Did some reading, but although Maggie can find satisfying companions and antagonists in words, I have always needed people—live ones. Thus Nantucket was my great relief, my great crossover, a true retreat from people, people, people.

Good letter from Mike—writes with words that touch me—

in thanks for something—and also relates that Connie is down, or up, to drinking beer in Germany.

Monday, April 11

Today Herb and Eddie and I had lunch. Instead of Press Club we went to the Biltmore just to celebrate. Eddie will be seventy on the 13th. He's a kid—the youngest of the original firm—so Herb and I gave him a two-volume Oxford Dictionary. Maggie suggested an inscription on the cover— With love and kisses or whatever we thought of to express affection, and then directions to see the pages referring to the words "Friend" and "Partner" with red ink arrows. Forty-five years come May we have shared—share and share alike— our skills with clients and our incomes. What a rare and perhaps unique experience. And no partners could have been more different in personalities, work habits or even specialties of interests in the law. Why they invited me to join I'll never know since they had good legal educations—which I did not— and they had worked in law offices and even written pleadings —which had not been part of my prior working life. Differences galore. Tempers at times, sulking at times—but like any great marriage the overriding glue was one of respect with disagreement, good will despite hasty words—and unbelievable forgiveness.

And from 1907 to 1914 my then advisers all told me not to study law at night and give up hope of practicing at the bar. I gambled and won. Never a regret at giving up $9,000 a year in 1914 to earn $500 the first ten months, $1,500 the next year and $3,500 the third year. I should have been a gambler at Deauville.

To dinner with Bill Astor at Carlton House. There I saw two of the most beautiful of women—the types that represent glamour to all the shop girls. I was awkward as usual with these samples from another world. They are not stupid—in fact have facile minds—but I never can find the subject matter of their conversations and keep staring at their perfection of hair-do, complexion, styles of clothing, jewelry. They are as entrancing as the unshaven bums in Washington Square—two sides of our cultural medallion—or is it the same side save for dollars and appearance?

Tuesday, April 12

It's many a moon since I have seen in a big city a moon like the one framed by 3rd Street last night at nine o'clock. Round, full and full of light. Strolled our village, dropping in for a moment at a poetry reading bar—sans liquor—minimum charge 75 cents. Wholesome and intellectually healthy even though sophisticates turn up their snob noses because the poets are not T. S. Eliot or even Emily Dickinson.

Wednesday, April 13

A wondrous batch of mail. Goodie [90] and Elizabeth [91] from London, Irving Kaufman, Helen Reid. Some days felicitous correspondence comes in big batches. Correlation!—buds are really, with vanity, covering the trees outside of our windows. It's natural that on such a day we note our recent barters— I have fallen at last for the use of Maggie's obnoxious paper handkerchiefs, and Maggie has been converted to showers in the morning.

Another great surprise. I read the galleys of Eisley's *Firma-*

[90] Arnold Goodman, London solicitor.
[91] Elizabeth Barber, Society of Authors, London.

ment of Time. It's a bit of velvet in my law practice that I get previews in galley form of new books. Here's one that hit me viscerally, in the spot where I was last attacked decades ago by James Harvey Robinson's *Mind In the Making.* This scholar can write from his peak of learning so that I can understand, and I actually feel myself getting out of my own limited frame of reference. So at night we try to make a list of the people we want to call into conference—the kid who invented the centerboard so that man need not sail only with the wind; the lad who converted a skid-log into the first wheel; the farmer who noted a crack in a stone in the field and associated it with frost; the scholar in 1675 who refused to believe that light traveled instantaneously; the woman or man who saw flat smooth stones on mountain tops and knew that wind can diminish peaks; and the imaginative person who saw the meaning of dirt flowing in streams into the oceans.

What a group to invite to a party! But similar observers are within our reach today and every day—alive and at our finger tips with new insights or farsights.

Thursday, April 14

Read *Poor Get Children,* an important study of ignorance as related to contraception in the low income families of our nation. Enjoyed Mary C.'s brief addendum.

Charmer comes in. Marital muss—please scare my husband —that's all he needs. How silly can adults be? Love through fright is unknown, affection by being "scared" impossible. So I explain—do you want docile acquiescence or can you put the bloom back on the peach? To reinstate life between two people takes some doing. Which reminds me that Einstein on a walk into the woods picked up a turtle for a grandchild, walked a few miles and then returned to put the turtle back where he found it, remarking, "I guess I've upset the universe enough!"

A judge has held that a poet reading poetry in our Square needs no speaker's permit. I assume that anyone reading poetry is immune—or does the freedom flow to the poet or to poetry? And why, although unusual and delightful, distinguish between a poem and an oration?

Letter received from U. of Mississippi. Could I help them locate famous etymologist and author Margaret Samuels Ernst. They desire her record for a Mississippi *Who's Who.* I wrote that I had heard of the dame and would try my best on their behalf.

Friday, April 15

Everyone astir about tax payments. Extension over Good Friday. Two more days for indecision and putting off a good duty to support our government—and buy our pieces of freedom and services which none can accomplish alone. It may be odd but I've never been irked by taxes, but only by increasing need of agents to pick up more pieces of change for the Federal Treasury. I suspect this polite blackmail is not the fault of the agents since they are led to believe, right or wrong, that promotions depend on additional assessments small enough to induce taxpayers to pay, even if unjustly, rather than hire a lawyer or an accountant.

Called Farnham to try once more to charter his Controversy 36-foot yawl in Maine with an option of purchase. Can't wait for Nantucket on June 1 and for July, on the Penobscot.

Can't figure out why the Dominican Republic newspaper ran the bitter attacks of the Burke articles in the *Times* in full, unedited, but with answers and explanations, or why the U.S. press did not take this as a first little sign of a debating press under Trujillo.

Sunday, April 17

Why do toe nails and hair grow more quickly and longer on males when very young and when very old?

I do observe. Whether precise or not it's a good observation. And what a mass of unobserved I live in. I remember the first time I observed the details of a horse's eye. Not all horse eyes are identical—Titian's father licked him if, after a stroll, he could not describe, always as unique, each and every horse he looked at. All are different, or each is different from all.

Happy at reviews of Mike Straight's new novel. He licked his burden of wealth and his father's greatness.

To Dave and Helen [92] in Irving's borrowed auto. Lovely house and tasteful home. Drove back on Thruway and did not get onto a wrong lane—and this for the first time.

To the Bernsteins' [93] for a cocktail party with many literate acquaintances—the Gelbs, Salisbury, the Ballantynes. Then to dinner with Amram and Dorothy.[94] Home early—still saddened by Knopf sellout to Random. And so Gresham's Law of Books pushes ahead. I'm sorry for Alfred and his stable of authors, the most distinguished in our land. In a decade mergers will reduce book publishing to five giants and a dozen true Editorial Publishers. What creative authors will be willing to be sandwiched between 500 or 1,000 titles—lives of a

[92] David Loth, author, and his wife.
[93] Theodore Bernstein of The *New York Times*.
[94] Amram Scheinfeld, anthropologist, and his wife.

Gabor or the like. The small house with fewer salesmen will still be preferred by the best of writers.

Tuesday, April 19

A man who came here as a child, spent all his decades of meaningful life in our land, was a member of the Communist Party for two or at most three years around 1938, has been ordered deported. Congress has so declared in a statute; and the Supreme Court in a divided opinion sustained the ejection of this human being. No report that I can find as to why he didn't join our nation and become a citizen.

This case continued to stay in my mind on and off. The Communist Party is a greater danger today in our nation than when McCarthy and Nixon beat the bushes and put many Americans into a debilitating fright. With Cuba and Panama close to Russian secret domination, we are in dire trouble, or at least freedom is in peril. But still law is not theory or rules. In the final analysis, is our great proud nation afraid of this man about to be cast out? Something is less than right.

In the evening to a gay stag party at Aly's home. Many illustrious people—mostly involved in worldwide affairs. I would have far preferred to grab any one of the group and have him all to my lonesome self. Exciting talks with David Owen,[95] groomed by Sir Stafford Cripps and who befriended me in London during the War during my trips on Trivia for F. D. R. Gracious buffet party.

[95] Of UN.

Wednesday, April 20

Maggie told me Steffie said she wanted a letter from me and remembered that I had once written her a letter. So I teased my correspondential ego and dropped the child a line.

Good heaven and temperature and the buds are breaking and the tassels are getting longer. Only forty days or so and we'll be in Nantucket—alone—all alone in the big house for a week or so. Jo and Delia may join us—this will be their thirty-fifth or thirty-sixth year as members of the family. Delia will not be able to work, but the grace of her gentle step more than pays for her food and roof. We all tread more lightly when she is with us. I'll be grateful to get off with Maggie—just a twosome.

In the evening the Beer [96] girls for dinner. Each with a different smile, each with a distinct twinkle of the eye and giggle—but much alike, even though not sisters but sisters-in-law.

Thursday, April 21

Nantucket weather and the tide on the East River is running down to the Harbor as I write, so the boats pass each other in different moods—one coasting, the other struggling.

Breakfast at Vanderbilt with Hiram, Tella and Roseman. Clearly the gap in standard of living will increase between India and the United States until at least 2035. Surely we as a people must stop wanting to be liked.

Letter from Al Stanford. He likes *Touch Wood* and may use parts in *Boats* magazine. I wrote him that I'm vain and enjoyed his flattery.

[96] Doris P. Beer, artist; Alice Beer of Peter Cooper Museum.

In the evening talked at AIGA [97] dinner on discrimination against creativity. Referred to preferentials on tariff, taxes, postage rates for all parts of our society except authors, photographers, painters and their publishers. Just no leadership in the Book profession, and the Authors Guild remains impotent—as is the case with all open-end unions.

Joe Martin reports Kirkpatrick of CIA admits Galindez was a CIA operator but suggests G. was let go because of woman trouble two years before his disappearance. If this is true Martin raised two questions: Who put up the quarter million dollars G. swore he received in the two years before his disappearance? And also, why did CIA snag $7,200 from the court, in secret fashion, so as to not leave a trace of the sum received and deposited by G. in his bank account in the forty-two days before he flew the coop.

Friday, April 22

Flew 8 A.M. jet to Chicago—one and a quarter hours. Recall parents worried about 20th Century Train of fifty years ago because of excessive speed—I think a mile a minute. On way chuckled at talk I had last night with Donald Adams of *New York Times.* "Kid Adams," I called him, for he has not even touched seventy. Will buy him a sport shirt lettered KID ADAMS —like a prize fighter of the mind. Enjoyed Edna B.[98] and husband—of Peter Pauper Press.

Read *What Is the Index* by Burke. Many surprises in list of banned books (none from U.S. since 1912) and area of fears of the R.C. Church.

In lighter fashion mused at reading that the sex of sea urchins is determined by temperature of the water. Good parlor game. Warm water produces more males or females?

[97] American Institute of Graphic Arts.
[98] Edna Beilenson.

Answer indicated by zoologist—we males need the higher temperature. What of bisexual urchins in lukewarm water? Not unlike lukewarm neuter parents in our society.

Most murders I learn are done by sane persons. My friend Gutmacher of Johns Hopkins so says—or so the press says he says.

Saw many old half-beaten friends in Chicago and at the ACLU Convention. Spoke at lunch in place of Ed Williams to Chicago lawyers on the people underserviced in legal representation if the cause or person is unpopular. We need 10,000 lawyers today to stand up to vigilantes, represent Negroes in the south, and so forth. Some judges give me reason to hope I started something at the luncheon.

Did two radio tapes for Illinois ACLU and one TV show and had vigorous chat with Don Moore and Charlie Liebman on the U.S. case *Monroe* vs. *Pape*. It's a honey of a case, and we have hope in high court unless they fear they will get too much work by allowing people who are arrested without cause at night and whose homes are searched without warrant to sue in a Federal Court—as citizens of U.S. as well as citizens of any state.

Home a little after midnight. Read Freud's *Totem and Taboo,* which Bennet sent me; looked at Rovere's new approach to Ike, and Adlai's sweet gracious phrases on Africa which I hate to admit comes out a little darker than ever.

Leaves out on our trees, water in pool in our park, apple tree across the street catches Maggie's eye.

Monday, April 25

Nature goes jerky—great unexpected heat. With amusement, nature enjoys watching the surprised discomfort of man.

Lunch with Sterling [99] and Ed Kuhn.[100] I may have discerned the way of letting laymen know of the Romance of the Law. Ed seemed interested in an eight- or ten-volume set of law cases with explanations in each volume treating a separate alley: censorship, libel, negligence cases, admiralty, privacy of the person, family law, and so forth. I'd enjoy being editor-in-chief—with an associate editor for each subject. I will want, if we close, to do the volumes on censorship, libel and privacy myself.

In the afternoon Jim Poling [101] dropped in. He wants to do a biography of my diluted gay world. I think I scared him off by telling him I have seventy bound volumes of notes and letters, from everyone from Rockefeller to F. D. R. to John L. to Carlo Tresca.

In the evening to talk on Barry Gray's radio program. Enjoyed Bob Joseph, the author-producer, and left Gingold and other stars to chat about the sad economic state of the theater, fast pricing itself out of the market by wastes of boondoggle and ice.

Friday, April 29

Last night, on reconsideration, I had two highlights—a speech on statesmanship by Carmine,[102] and a stirring talk by a relaxed Averell Harriman. He should have fired his speech writers when campaigning against Rockefeller.

Today at Saints and Sinners luncheon, Harry Golden was the Sinner and did a neat job in reply to those clever personality surgeons—Harry Hershfield and O'Rourke.

[99] Sterling Lord, literary agent.
[100] Editor at Macmillan.
[101] Jim Poling, author and free lance writer.
[102] De Sapio, N. Y. Democratic leader.

Closed exciting big publishing house matter—exciting because it needed many legal inventions.

Sad news and good tidings about the Goldies. Their beautiful—in face and spirit—Jamaican maid, Allaner, will have another child and must quit work for a while. Tough for Joan to interview new ones.

Saturday, April 30

Lunch at Commodore Hotel at alumni meeting of New York Law School, which I attended from 1909 to 1912 five nights a week—at night all of fall, winter and spring. It was a good school—everyone was in earnest—much like the seriousness of the G.I. students after World War II. Many judges and eminent attorneys were at the luncheon—the dean spoke of trying to get this school into the front ranks of the great Eastern law schools. A sad ambition. Better that his law school start a *new* front—one where lawyers do not seek striped pants but may want to serve people and lead the republic. Attorney General spoke graciously with humor. Clear to me why he can get votes. And still a sad affair— no sense of greatness.

Twenty-five years ago we bought our first small car, now the automaking leaders at last have come around to small cars. Maybe some day the movie tycoons will see that the people do enjoy good foreign pictures and let them get into theater chains—not just in a few big-city small art theaters. And finally some day the TV networks may—but late—wake up to the real desires of people, just as the auto manufacturers have done on size of cars.

Home. Fixed dinner—good browned potatoes, crabmeat with cream sauce, pie—and to bed.

May

Sunday, May 1

Read Kavanaugh's *Hermeneutics of Kadnaminsha* explaining his library adventure in relation to his early schooling in Ireland. It's a delight to read.

Maggie's new publisher Leonard Harris came over to work on new version of *In A Word*, originally published before the war by Knopf. Happy—new edition with new words.

Went over a smear campaign in New York *Post*. It's a dirty campaign, as were the Hoover, Leibowitz series. So much that is valid could be written about all public characters that it's hard to explain why—just why—a team of five reporters is assigned by the *Post* to dig only below the waist. There is scarcely a valid blow or fair criticism—most of the articles are inferences, innuendoes and indecencies. Peculiarly sad, since Wechsler, Fleeson, Childs, Lerner and Porter are at times our most illuminating liberal commentators.

For dinner at Rickey's with Lena and Ellen and Zelda Dorfman—and all of us to City Center to see *Finian's Rainbow*. A better production than the original—music, dance and dialogue more full of mirth than anything I have seen on Broadway in years.

Monday, May 2

Main event—drinks with Maggie Cousins whom I picked up at her office and then off to Park Lane. She bought one essay, and I handed her an outline of another. Some day I must read this magazine with its six and a half million readers—or is it more? Our talk roamed, as all chatter does between five and seven over cocktails. Much less concentrated than at luncheon or dinner. More of the nature of the talk between my bride and me in bed over coffee every morning as we read our papers. Went from variety of size, color and maturity of stars to right of privacy in letters written by nonliterary folk to friend or foe, to telepathy and the universal desire of all men and women to play with anything supernatural. As I put her in a cab I said, "I guess you want a hunk of immortality." Some remark, considering the hazards of Park Avenue traffic.

In evening Maggie watched a Shaw TV play, and I went over some of her new words for the revised edition of *In A Word*.

Thursday, May 5

On and off during the day I recalled reading that in some theology it was taboo to carry an open umbrella. Odd—can't dream of a reason. Confused as when in Italy, church-going women must have hats or shawls covering their heads, wear shoes, dress with sleeves. Not unlike hats for men in Jewish worshipping buildings—and still none of the founders of old religions had shoes or hats in those hot climates.

In evening, Alan and new-hair-do-Paula for dinner. After, the Schaffer twins dropped in. The one who wrote hit show *Five Finger Exercise* looks like a barrister—the other doesn't, but is. Around midnight Connie and Mike and von Auw—quiet, always bemused agent—and an Italian agent who thinks all of our culture is beneath contempt, dropped in.

Happy with news that I have Farnham's yawl in Maine for July. Late to bed. Moon sharp and clear and trees are shining.

Friday, May 6

Thurber introduction to Maggie's new revised *In A Word* is wonderful, gracious and tender.

Played with Maine Coast charts—designing cruise day by day. Maybe the white sand in Roque Island once more this summer.

Saturday and Sunday, May 7 and 8

Startled by good news items in science magazines. Three brains of man—reptilian, lower mammal (that is, mouse to man), and the third, mind of man—must write to National Institute of Mental Health for details; then from California a new trick for testing age to 100,000 years by 800° F. heat—Carbon 14 only gave us 40,000 years of history; in Japan papers are actually being sent by facsimile over the air—40 pages a day and for distances of 600 miles.

For lunch to Guggenheim Museum. Great building, functionally exciting and the public in its highest state of giggles at the pictures and more particularly at the titles chosen by modern artists. Then to World Trade Show at Coliseum, where audience was in high glee. No cynicism or disdain and above all great showing of identification with cultures of origin. Heard only Spanish at exhibits from Spain.

In evening to see Thurber movie *Battle of the Sexes*—once more Sellers and England made a good movie which all women going in to male professions should see at an early age.

Letter from R. L.—signed by him—from home. I hope he goes to his office before summer or his high conscience may let him believe he is not needed at 23 Wall. He's needed, and, moreover, I hate to think of him retired at seventy-eight. Too young a mind, too old and basic an integrity of thought.

Monday, May 9

Dreary weather can't make up its mind between rain and clearing.

Lunch with Phil Scharper of Sheed & Ward. Discussed methods of preventing nasty public stir in newspaper if the accusations of Protestant and Jewish doctors become public. They complain in many places that Catholic Hospitals are harassing non-Catholic doctors on their individual right to prescribe contraceptives or work with Planned Parenthood

Federation. Then to problem of *Pamela*—used for students at Catholic College even though on R.C. Index. This can be confusing if reported—our press generally garbles such items. Maybe worthwhile for publisher to move to get *Pamela* off the Index—not an unusual proceeding. In fact, I guess that at the next Ecumenical Congress the Index itself may be entirely abandoned as a worn-out instrument.

Tuesday, May 10

Sun up, and people are rather pleasant. But all seem troubled by shameful, ineffective lies told to the people of our nation on the mystery of the plane brought down in Russia. Spying is conceded—immoral but necessary. Is lying immoral if used to deceive Russia? Above all, getting caught in a cheap stupid lie has hurt us throughout the world and, worse yet, in our own self-esteem. I guess it may be all to the good. CIA, even under a good citizen like Allen Dulles, must be inefficient, corrupt and stupid—because his power is too great. We must get the CIA to be part of our government and report at least to the Chairmen of the House and Senate Committees, as the Atomic Energy Commission does.

And today Clauson and Hutcheson of CIA call Joe Martin and Santori of the *Daily News* liars when they repeat Kirkpatrick's statement of last week that G. worked for the CIA. What a nasty world with a cowardly press. The *News* sees no story in G. working for the CIA and then disappearing—only a story, they will say, if the mystery of G.'s disappearance is solved. What a press!! And this is the bravest of them all.

Wrote to Hugo Black to see if he is agreeable to a new biography by Atheneum. I reviewed the good one written a decade ago by John Frank, the Justice's former secretary.

But Black has become clearer and firmer on liberty of individuals.

Orthodox Jewish rabbis run an advertisement objecting to discrimination against Jews. Guess where—Israel!

To Bar Association annual meeting—not vigorous for the minds, the good minds present. Then to "21" to meet Peyton Ford and his Mrs. for a snifter. First time late at night at "21" in moons. In olden days up there three nights a week with Heywood, Thurber, Benchley and that engaging heavy-drinking and light-talking crew.

Wednesday, May 11

Even in the days of Marco Polo, the planet was not put through such a squeezer. Today I read a pamphlet by Hitson and Funkenstein of Harvard on family patterns and para-noidal personality in Boston and Burma. Who could resist such an article? The aggression in Burma, I learn, turns out-ward—not so in Boston. They conclude that there are system-atic relationships between types of family culture and forms of mental illness. I read, regretfully, much that reduced my affectionate image of competent, serene and smiling Burmese women.

Hubert H. out of presidential race. I don't know why, but to most people he didn't seem like a President.

Worked at home on outline of leadership of Judge Warren who, unlike Hughes, does not press for unanimity; unlike Felix F. does not use mystic legal vernacular; and, unlike many of the judges, believes that law does, must and should flex with societal changes.

Tempted to buy a new six-foot catamaran. Teasing myself. It's only $50 but I need an excuse. Will Nick and Steffie use it? If the amount is unreasonable and great, I make decisions with ease and without any pressures from secret corners of thought. But $50—I must toy with the idea—like $2 for a pair of socks, or a $2.50 face lotion.

Thursday, May 12

Getting restless for Nantucket. Catalogues of Abercrombie & Fitch and boat chandleries are now my favorite reading.

This morning for breakfast at the home of Cardinal Spellman with Leon.[103] Pleasant and with frank areas of disagreement. Will send to the Cardinal my present hopes for a statement derived from my Harold Gardiner dinners. Also will get position more clearly of the Church with respect to the Index and more particularly as to *Pamela*. Must send the Cardinal my paper on the Colombia, S.A. literacy miracle.

Why won't the noble proponents of birth control meet with Catholics of good will? Is it insecurity? Is it a fear of being persuaded? I think not. Is it the general tendency of man to think that issues as well as people are either black or white, when surely life is loaded down with all the in-between hues and shades?

Gracious note from Jim Bennett to whom I wrote in nonprofessional terms for transfer of Costello from Atlanta to near his wife. He didn't say yes, and he didn't say no. Odd for a nonwobbly person.

Friday, May 13

Shocked to hear over the radio last night that Aly had been killed in an auto accident in Paris. Ran right up to Pakistan

103 Leon Lowenstein, cotton goods merchant.

House and to Aly's apartment to give comfort. Aly was a rare and, for me, odd friend. We understood each other for years with ease. I still thank Bill Astor for asking me up for breakfast years ago to counsel with Aly.

It's sad. Aly was just being reborn on this earth. He was entering a new life. He played hard and worked hard—a way of life not practiced, and certainly not understood, in our society. Our playboys become bums and our working men don't ever really learn how to play and relax. I treasured his affection and confidence.

Today thought of little else, and the only item in the public prints that retraveled my brain paths was not the President's ineptness on the spy issue or the further evidence of Communist take-over of the Castro dictatorship but *The New York Times* story that Ike does not read the daily papers and, in quotes, "I normally read only the Sunday papers." How better point up loss of stature that he has brought to our great nation.

Saturday, May 14

Met Maggie at Parke-Bernet auction rooms to see the Dufys—none in oil. Remained for auction—an experience I last had possibly forty-five years ago during my only period as a collector. I still have some of those Zorn etchings. But my failure to remember the conventions or law of the Auction Room nearly cost me $1,000. Across the aisle I saw and waved to Harold Clurman and, I assumed, his new bride. The auctioneer thought my wave meant a bid for the Gainsborough painting which I would not even want to live with.

In evening to a Japanese movie—well acted and great beauty in photography but agree with Maggie that this is a difficult folkway to understand.

Received a letter from a friend of Connie's in Massachusetts—a friend of thirty years ago. All it said was: "You helped
me once before when I was desperate. I'm desperate again.
I need you. Will you repeat your help?" So I called her up,
and she was embarrassed. Sad that man is so out of tune
that a proffer of help appears as a shock of unnatural and
unusual portent.

Sunday, May 15

Usual two-hour-long hot bath, with iced coffee on ledge,
inflated pillow (it gets too hot) under my head and the two
book sections. Many books do I enjoy reading about, but
only few *must* I read, and those most often for needed knowledge. Of recent years—since meeting Marie—mostly in the
field of human science. I was shocked when I realized the
number of words I write a year—nearly a million in notes,
memos, letters, articles and books. About 300,000 words in
daily diary notes and memos on travels; law articles, 200,000;
letters daily about 5,000 words a week, mostly not with any
concerned or attempted grace; and then also articles or
fiction stories for magazines—not to mention a book every
year or so—100,000 words. It sounds quite silly and certainly
futile. But only a small portion is due to external pressures,
such as perfunctory answering of letters that should not have
been written in the first place. And the President of our
nation does not read much, if anything!

In the afternoon strolled to Bessies' to see Nick's baseball-
black eye; in park on way back saw Judge Valenti sitting on
bench warming himself out of a cold. In the evening for
dinner with Edna Ferber and the Boakums; Mr. B., a gay
laughing 75 and Mrs. B. (Fanny Butcher) of Chicago book
store and critic fame—truly worth revisiting again.

Back to Ferber's, but since she has no TV set left early to watch Nixon being interviewed by Susskind. Soon left for bed—bored by dull discussion which should well have been "closed-end." What a chance D. S. had and flubbed. He didn't know the difference between conversation and cross-examination or, if he did know, failed to realize the first test of cross-questioning: don't ask witness a question unless you are damn sure of his answer. D. S. was so unprepared and amateurish that Nixon properly treated him like a school boy who deserved sympathy and help on his commencement oratory. This later was E. F.'s good simile. And the Monday *Times* gives it front page under a by-line. Why did not *Times* get R. N. for an interview? Must local TV stations rate higher than our best paper?

Monday, May 16

Forty-five years ago yesterday the four of us opened a law office at 2 Rector Street.

Party this afternoon. Meaningless to most of the staff even though Ethel, our first and only employee of 1915 is still here, and Paula and May Frier have suffered with us for more than thirty-eight years. It's a lifetime of success, pleasure and a basketful of errors and faulty decisions. In balance the plus far exceeds the minus, and I dare say no other partners have carried on at the bar in this big city for such a period of time.

Some of the alumni dropped in. Everyone agreed our most acute error was getting too big—about twenty-five lawyers. Some day I'll see if I can find the optimum size for a law office with respect to happiness, craftsmanship and take home pay after taxes. How I'd love to go back to 1915— erase the past and see if I would have made the same stupid decisions or grabbed the same flotsam of luck that went across my desk. Other partners gave the three of us beautiful, gold desk clocks.

Tuesday, May 17

The rate of prison population increase is frightening, but so far no one has dramatized the evils of people held in jail uselessly before trial, and new experiments have not even been publicly discussed. Does sex starvation in jails do more than distort the personalities of distorted men and women; why should not all prisoners—other than those who commit mayhem or peddle drugs or arms—be allowed to work off their debts but sleep in jails; why should not teachers in jails be the preferred educators in our land—certainly they have the most backward pupils; why should not unions be removed from their selfish control of industries in jails? So many whys and we are getting nowhere at all.

Dinner with the Donald Adamses and the Beilensons at 2 Fifth. Adams came in with the sweat shirt I sent him—with "Kid Adams" lettered across his chest. I enjoy small hoaxes.

Friday, May 20

Read *Science Is Never at War*, with its dramatic chapter on Ben Franklin as ambassador in Paris giving passports for increase of human knowledge to scientists irrespective of their positions, if any, in pending wars. What a different world today when science is government-financed for the purpose of national security which in part depends on secrecy.

Good letters from Judge Black and R. L. who is reading and writing with his healthy insights. In regard to my "Year 2000" project, he writes:

Dear Morris:

Thank you for your letter of May 11th and the enclosed paper about the widening income gap between the rich and poor nations. I promise not to write you a twenty-page letter which you say I did about Bigness, partly because I am still enfeebled after my operation. But I can give you the headliness of my thought, for what little they may be worth to you. I have two difficulties: one is that the thought that runs through this paper has a trend to egalitarianism. I am strongly for foreign aid but I do not think that envy on the part of the poor or shame on the part of the rich is a good basis for it. I think we ought to help the poor because they need our help. I think our wealth will make it easier for us to help them, and indeed, without anything being done about it at all, our growing wealth and trade will help the poorer nations, not hurt them. So I am not much interested in exploring the question whether the rich are growing richer, though I am interested in exploring the question what we can do to help the poor to feed themselves.

My second difficulty is that you seem to be in such an awful hurry about it. It took us in the western world 200 or 300 years to achieve a flowering of the industrial revolution, although we started on a much higher level than the unfortunate people of Asia and Africa are starting from. I think it is a mistake to try to industrialize the people of the East or the South in a hurry. Sudden wealth has not helped much the unfortunate people of Persia or Iraq or Saudi Arabia. Despots like the Communists of Russia and China, who don't hesitate to starve off or otherwise liquidate their surplus population, may be able through the exercise of their despotic power to accelerate the industrialization of their countries, but steel plants and oil fields will never feed the more or less democratic people of agrarian and nomadic countries who are still friendly to us or at least neutral. I think we should be helping the poor and backward countries to improve their agricultural and pastoral economies. I have the impression that the Fords and Rockefellers have been doing good work in this field.

Yours ever,
RUSSELL

Sunday, May 22

Have approached diary notes with little enthusiasm—not that nothing happens or too much happens. With days of rain I am at a period of loss of energy. I miss Heywood and R. L.

Tuesday, May 24

Slept late and lolled at home with Maggie. Weather down. Cousins sends back a piece ordered by *McCall's* with suggestions for changes—which I'll try to understand, feeling sure she is more right, as editor, than I can ever be. Read that science has found in the brain of man one cubic inch that ties in to the heart. I mean the real heart—the great pump that is far better than any General Electric or Motors engine. It is not the heart of the poets, of love, of passion or tenderness. It's odd that a pump should be identified with love and affection.

Thursday, May 26

Up to office with Mike and then strolling up Park Avenue ran into three top publishing officials. On the corner of 39th we talked, working out a program—or what in other words is called "doing business." I like street corner conferences in the early morning before the rush of opening office mail and getting bogged down by that damnable modern instrument called a telephone. At the office a half hour later, these three competent editors will become organizational men and hence futile except for interoffice memos.

Friday, May 27

Finished an article with Bonn on my experiment at Williams, and at U. of Texas, of awards by students to teachers. Hope it can be marketed by Alan Collins' [104] gal, Miss Jacobson.

Excited by client who comes in with story of Nazi captured by Israel. What a tale for Drew Pearson to put into a book and 20th Century to use on the silver screen.

Heard from Frederick of Ford about the excitement my memo on the Year 2000 has created.

Last real day at office—tomorrow Nantucket opening packages, cleaning shells off pier, launching boats and, best of all, looking with affection on our piece of land, real home, and the trees we planted more than thirty years ago.

So as I leave the Square for the Harbor I weigh in at 175.

Saturday, May 28 and Sunday, May 29

To Idlewild for small plane to Nantucket. For the first time in about thirty-five years neither Jo nor Delia comes with us—but Maggie has little trouble getting responsible, likeable help. With Jo not here Maggie has to point out all of our minor household traditions which Jo passed on from

[104] Head of Curtis Brown, literary agents.

person to person. My little morning, home-carved coffee pot stand; our techniques for passing out breakfast and luncheon food to the terrace through the hall off the kitchen; iced coffee in big pot day and night.

Much to fix and repair: the inside-outside thermometer, the barometer to be wound and inked, pier to be swept of gull shells, step the mast, bend the sail, put up sign posts—innumerable caretaker chores, all of which I care for and cherish. They call for minor skills of electric wiring, plumbing and carpentry. At once I try out the tools in the shop—cut a step for Mike's new wing (probably cut it too small for the screen door to ride it semi-circle).

Town is quiet and empty. Weather sunny and crisp. With delightfully weary muscles, to bed early and to sleep while reading the first page of a new book on Stonehenge.

New York seems far away in time and space. The big window frames a new world—the Brant Point shore. No one along our shore except Mary H.; [105] the beach has not been much changed; little if any building during the winter; the boat strike is serious but no one is frenetic about it. Time of tide is important, and the temperature in and out—and the barometer must be at hand. Here if I don't have a screwdriver, knife, marlin spike, pliers in reach, I feel as if I have lost a hand. My problems are small, intimate, soluble and nothing of national or international import seems much worth thinking about.

Monday, May 30

Another bright day and all our muscles—too long unused—are aching. They feel as if they are angry at me for deserting them all winter—the most irritated are toward the rear of

[105] Hettinger, neighbor.

the lower legs. But we keep on—build a new rose lattice, with Maggie doing the tie backs, for I have never learned to get along with thorns.

Downtown to see the Memorial Day Parade come up Union to Broad to Main to the cemetery—the same parade for thirty years, down to the tots at the rear holding a few wilted lilacs in their hands.

The town seems spiritually aroused by the boat strike. "We took care of ourselves during the Revolution and the War of 1812; we will stand up against the strikers' demands." All reasonable since the pay-scale of the boatline workers, never made public before, now shows that the annual take-home pay of men on the boats is far above that of the workers on either the Vineyard or Nantucket.

Put new treads on brow to pier, fixed up shop with thousands of goodies which I'll never use, but if one is needed in a hurry all my stingy hoarding (like the old lady with her bits of string) will bring an emotional reward of unappraisable value. Up and down Main Street—a friendly word here, a thanks for our letter about the school fight, a brief chat with the astronomer, Miss H.,[106] who with cheer still deplores the great number of stars in our heaven.

Didn't know I was tired when I left town, but now it's proven by my ease at napping and my sleep at night running four or five hours more than in New York. The office and 2 Fifth just crossed my mind for the first time and then scooted away after a fleeting jiffy.

Tuesday, May 31

To Allen's for dinner—crowded for this time of year, and ran into many of town friends. The talk is of school and boat

[106] Margaret Harwood.

strike. In the midst of troubles this town can talk misery but never with a mood of catastrophe. Up here the excitements are different—none of the restlessness of the Broun-Benchley types who always, to their dying days, thought that the beer would be better in the next bar. It never was. They didn't care, nor even appraise. All they needed was an excuse for change, for moving on. Up here, as in most of our towns of livable size, people are more likely to believe in what they do; whereas in New York—even in our unique law office—so few do more than a little of what they believe in.

Our first foggy, dour day. So kept busy, though old age threatened—shown by reluctance to swim before breakfast when thermometer is at 50, barometer dropping and dew is cold on pier and grass. But my feet cotton to the sand, grass and pebbles. Care little about cigarettes, and certainly no greed for chainsmoking forty a day. I'm so busy doing what in the City I would call "nothing" that I have not gotten around to finishing the essay ordered by *McCall's* nor cared enough about the robbery of our liquor and other items to call up the State Police. Is this lethargy, living or lack-adaisicalness? It's good for me—but for how long, who knows?

June

No date—no day—but first part of June

Up here I write my diary note at no regularized time. Coming in from the garden or the waterfront I'm apt to write a line or two. Result: I haven't the faintest idea if I have written a diary note for each day this week. Nor is there any distinguishing event. The morning fog rolls out in midmorning and the rain has been so stingy that the deeper roots must turn upward in prayer—tantalized by having a few drops seep down at most two or three inches.

But the island is loveliest now and in late September. We drive the Sconset circuit—chat at post office with victualer Clem Reynolds of the fancy hats.

In the elm tree the battle continues between the beetle and the woodpecker. The beetle is eaten by the woodpecker but is also grateful to it for the pecker makes the holes in which the beetle enjoys living and eating. This is more interesting and more easily discernible than if they were of one family. Many a father and son among humans ride the same circuit; but the pain is less physical and the cannibalism is only of emotions.

Wednesday, June 1

Between cutting grass, which brought me many satisfactions—not least of which was the ability or luck I had in starting our gasoline cutter—and setting outhaul off the float to place the dinghy, I kept busy. Over the winter, a dentist-type tree surgeon, retained to nurse the apple and the elm trees, cut away my favorite 40-foot branch from the apple. This made grass cutting easier—less scratching up of my balding head—but the kids will miss it for climbing and now, regrettably, we can see up our private inroad. One must tell dentists, tree doctors and in fact all men of the drill and knife, the precise limits of their duties. With a knife or a drill in hand the discoverer in man takes over, always digging a little further to see what's there—a sort of diminutive Everest complex. It's not unlike my chisel when I have a block of wood on the lathe. The great art is stopping just before it's finished rather than just after.

Maggie's books arrived—so a new shelf of about forty volumes is resting, inviting our attack. Before kids and company, after a few hours of labor I rest and read—anything that's in arm's reach. I guess I finish a book a day during these early empty weeks—not in a heat as in my youthful rampages at college, when I rushed to the old library and read a play a day sitting in the same chair at the very same table.

Our favorite catbird is back with us promptly for bread—no carrots, no peas, no lettuce. Very choosey. It takes a day or so for her to overcome fear of movable strangers; but she's already up on the table and by tomorrow will eat out of our hands.

The office is far away in space and time—though I got an immediate restorative to my professional life when Alan called to say that Kookie,[107] Hewes [107a] and others may come up to discuss my plan for ending the Equity dispute on an affirmative level. But at once back to the iris at the gate, the screen that needs a new hanger, and fixing a lamp wiring in the maid's bedroom.

Thursday, June 2

Built a road sign for Ed. W.; [108] got him a car for his stay here and tried to charter a TV set for his use during the Democratic Convention. It's my guess the Republican Convention may be the real gay affair—with Nelson R. getting the ovation of the year.

We went for a sail—the Nicholie in good shape, all varnished, new side rail and new halyards. No boats out. Few if any homes on water front opened up.

Maggie's flowers came from Oliver so she will be busy all day planting. This is her one hobby. Reading is not a hobby with her—it's her life. Not to have a book in her hand is like not having a hand.

To dinner at Beers' gallery home on North Wharf—with Don Tilghman and Alice B. Smoked as if I were in New York—chimney fashion. Since arrival I haven't used up more

[107] Edward Kook, lighting expert.
[107a] Of *Saturday Review*.
[108] Edward Bennett Williams, lawyer-author.

than a package of cigarettes. But last night, although discussion was neither serious nor violent, and we were merely prospecting the future of the island and art and our nation, I found myself smoking one cigarette after another. It's odd —when I concern myself only with the present, it seems that I need not smoke at all. The problems of the moment, the issues solved by hands, create no such tension as tobacco will relieve. It isn't even tobacco—it's just grabbing for something to stick in my mouth, like Eddie who handles in idle fashion a dry, empty pipe all day long.

Sunday, June 5

Rainy so just didn't take a dip before breakfast, but down to good food. Arlene will delight the kids. Cakes, cookies and craftsmanship—she is so good because she enjoys her job. Puttered in shop—a world-important chore (that is, to my own tiny, present world of this day, the 5th of June).

Gazed for four minutes at the catboat to enjoy a new stunt of mine. Copper bottom paint certainly keeps off underwater life so that the bottom does not readily become cluttered with barnacles. But everyone knows that the worst of the muck attached itself to the boat at the precise waterline—that is, the place where copper bottom paint ends and noncopper, topside paint begins. So, despite convention, I painted the copper paint three or four inches above the waterline. Now must keep an eye on it to see how it works— the only difference is a trained eye may see the bottom paint extending up the side a few inches.

Cut hedge at shower, filled kerosene can for heater, started to gather implements, log for Maine cruise. Anticipation and experience for me are more consuming than memories.

Monday, June 6

Anticipating trip to New York so had a less restful night. There, problems involve other people—whose lives are to a lesser or greater degree affected by my wisdom or lack of it. Here nobody is touched by our daily exercises in living. So I give a parting glance at innumerable things we made—objects that are unknown in other homes, items we enjoy. For example, what other home has a special custom-built double shelf to hold ice-coffee jug and place for bamboo glasses underneath, an antique-appearing bracket curved to fit a cheap but now irreplaceable alarm clock; a maple turned holder for pencils with a mahogany lathed penholder on my desk. Each room has at least one result of our awkward skills with carpenter tools—all unaccustomed to our hands until thirty-five years—or half our lifetimes—ago.

Monday, June 6 thru Thursday, June 9

Off on noon plane on request to discuss, not the Actors' strike, but what can be done about the economics of the theater. Good food and talk at the Kookies'. The next great step is to recapture for those who are in the theater—performers, technicians, producers, designers and investors—the $5 to $10 million now pirated by treasurers and representatives of producers. After an opening all reviews are read at 4 A.M. *The New York Times,* no matter who the critic, can close any show by an unfavorable notice. This does not mean that a favorable review will make a hit, but the *Times* and any two other dailies give a sound gamble, and the treasurer of the theater can tell his wife or friend to open that secret tin box and bring $5,000 to the theater when the office opens in the morning. In exchange, $5,000 worth of tickets—a neat little pocket-size package—is handed out. These are the tickets that sell for $20 or $30 apiece depending on the degree of the hit—that is, the demand for tickets by the rich or the large companies that entertain their own officials and customers at the expense of the U.S. Treasury to the extent of at least half of the cost. If we could get these millions into the theater then pension plans and wage scales would be worthy of reconsideration. Now all the strike does is try to divide a deficit (except for a few hits). The owners of the hits are not the owners of the current flops—hence no real averaging by investors is possible on any realistic terms.

On way to New York had a chat with Mrs. Nat Benchley about theaters and writer troubles in Hollywood. I suggested that when Nat gets his next bid to "write" a movie he should make a contract to bring his own crew of five or six writers rather than be handed five strangers—who don't know each other's aptitudes, who fight for kudos, and who of necessity create less than a well-adjusted working team. Nat could turn out better words, dialogues and action at far less cost and far more, more profit and joy to himself.

After Kookies' went to Bessies' until far too late.

Next morning at Goldies' for breakfast—all well. Later in day, voted for the regular Democratic ticket in primary; stopped to see our ever-expanding Washington Square art show; used up three stenographers on mail; back at Bessies' for Kathie's birthday party; and then to dinner with Monsignor Flynn by arrangement of Cardinal Spellman. We talked frankly about the censorship problems, and birth control debates in U. S. Supreme Court, hospitals, and so forth. Surely the Catholics, less than the Protestant sects, caused enactment of Birth Control laws in 1870's. But now I understand why the Catholic Church has declined to do more than stay silent on the efforts to repeal. With some luck I should be able to get a Catholic lawyer on our brief in the Connecticut Birth Control Case in the Supreme Court to make clear the Catholic position: that the Church needs no laws in a Catholic culture, it does not care to interfere with freedom of choice of techniques for non-Catholics, and hence remains silent in the debates on repeal or constitutionality.

Next day stands out because I went up to have dinner with Russell, whom I found in fine spirits. Just the two of us in his large, elegant home. He is less lonely than I would be, because he is a more self-sufficient person. We roamed from the delights he found in Felix Frankfurter's *Reminiscences,* to the value of a joke book—such as I discussed with George Britt over cocktails—showing jokes for, of, by, and against different nations, cultures, and occupations.

Up at dawn, gathered Nicholas and Steffie—with Irv taxiing us to plane—and took the kids to Nantucket. What a joy for me to watch their memory glands being titillated. A house, a fence, a store, a whale skull, the garden—each tickled their brains. But best of all they ran off to see their own homes on either side of our house where they will remain until the parents come next week.

Friday, June 10

Hard cold N.E. wind. Read my favorite science magazines to learn that southern birds are flying further north, particularly mockingbirds and turkey vultures. Does this mean changes in temperature, just more adventure, less food on usual routes, or that birds get acclimated, as does man?

Man has found an untarnishable silver—a kind of Argalin process. Years ago I was quite involved, on behalf of silver-

135

smiths, in the proper markings: "filled," "plated," "sterling." The tarnish problem was always the retarding factor in sales —folk want shiny splendor but not the arduous use of chamois and elbow grease.

Then I considered sovereignty of the air. How high up should a nation have exclusive rights to air. Sputnik I and several Discoverers fly around, at 10 to 600 miles above our earth—the differences between perigees and apogees of orbits. As the cameras get improved, the problems of interference in views from the air will change. Good problem for international lawyers to take their minds off their main concern: How can big corporations avoid tariff and tax burdens of all nations?

Not yet at ease and rested—those two days in the office were a great jar. Maybe as I get older, enjoying my two separate diets of life—my City and Nantucket—I will find the transports of spirit from one to the other more trying. As yet the stress is greater from the Big City to the Island rather than the other way around. Don't understand it.

Saturday, June 11

Today Gib Waine, the electric wizard, came over to talk Boat Strike with me. He let me know that my name had been suggested at an Authority meeting as an arbiter.

The old anemometer hovers between 25 and 35 knots all day. It's bleak and hard out. All this made me feel lazy— and what with disturbing national news, I have been on the dull side. Have we no friends in Japan to make answer to the Communist-led opposition to the visit of our President? Or are our people men of minor emotional key, and less given to parades and physical conflict? Is this the pattern to be expected from the intelligent and rational as compared to the ignorant and emotional? Cuba is another story—there we were led by Herbert Matthews to our present intolerable debacle. Months ago, at the Overseas Press Club, he said we should be patient while the revolution wiped out the middle class—an operation that did not seem to meet with his disfavor.

Monday, June 13

Sun at last, so off in the sailing vessel with Nick and Stef right after breakfast, but first got Nick to row the boat all alone up and down the shore—after he first said he couldn't do it. He found at once that he was wrong—hence was entranced—which is what youth needs most when viewing the full, unbelievable capacities of adult man. Standards of attainment are essential, for if they are well planted, security becomes less important.

This is my island life once more—with lunch in the garden which, in a wind from the west or north quadrant, is always much warmer in the mornings facing the rising sun. A few cruising families sailed in over the week end but weighed anchor early this morning. In two weeks I'll be in Maine cruising the Penobscot.

Reread parts of Bolitho's *Twelve Against the Gods*—enjoyed the Isadora Duncan one—the girl and family who felt that society owed her a living with extravagance. She was too independent to accept it from a husband or lover—or even a paying public. Rarely did the butcher and candlestick-maker offend her by asking that bills be paid. Lola Montez was sheer driving will power. Even kings had to give way to her bewitching drive. Although these two ladies each had many lovers, they were still neurotic enough to need a couch more than I suspect they ever really enjoyed a double bed.

Took Nick through some new routines—putting up screens and measuring for screw eyes and hooks, cutting brackets on jigsaw for shelves for his new playroom. My standards are not high enough to scare him off.

Tuesday, June 14

The impulse to contrive is worthy of one of the greater graces. It has beauty in its lowest outlets. Today a new metal basket came for Nick's bicycle. It didn't fit and we had to figure out what to do. Cut it down, bore holes, flatten ends— so Nick and I contrived with metal drill, metal saw. It worked —its utility and cost of minimal concern.

Wednesday, June 15

Played with my kind of Penguin book—*Riddles in Mathematics* by Northrup. Had fun with Maggie on old-time puzzles and then tried a few on Nick.

Read of Daphne's [109] death. We were sad. She was such a beautiful lady—outward looks and inward feelings. I don't know what kind of a life Max will have without her. Last we saw them was out West a year or so ago and this memory and others are rich for both of us.

Thursday, June 16

Sad day for U.S.A. It seems to me to be the inevitable result of the Eisenhower political philosophy—all govern-

[109] Daphne Drake Mason.

ment activity is to be deplored. There is to him no large area of behavior which individuals cannot provide for themselves. Government activity must be minimized and deprecated. Hence, personal government is in favor—a method for reducing organized government as a human means for the joint efforts of millions of separate people who are impotent one by one. Today Ike gets his second, separate personal rebuff. Mr. K. at Paris, and now the K-inspired mob in Japan, forces the government to tell Ike to stay home. So by his own attitude toward the philosophy of government he invites *personal* rebuffs; and it may take us a long time before a president again tries to act as a personal salesman of good will. Ike's own good will is not enough—even though his accent on the individual did not arise out of conceit but only out of ignorance of the role of government.

It's sad—as populations increase and governments comprise ever larger areas, we have lived through seven years of preaching "Beware of Government," "Do It All Yourselves," "Through Government You Lose Your Freedom," and such like. This when, in fact, the peace of the world depends on relations between governments and not, as Norman Cousins and other dreamboys cry out, between peoples. Peoples—illiterate and isolated—want peace of course; but mere desire is of little help when the instruments of peace are as complicated as tariffs and trade—to mention simple ones. Few mortals have the skills needed to work out the techniques.

Maybe the Democrats will understand the great danger of government too big in some areas and the need for more powerful government in international matters.

Joan, Irv, Alma [110] and Boots [111] arrived during a few sun

[110] Alma Johnson, maid.
[111] Cat.

spots that broke the clouds. Steffie sad when plane missed the field, and then high in joy when they flew in with Steve [112] from Hyannis on small plane. The clan is gathering.

Sunday, June 19

Back into Nantucket weather—breakfast in garden after my swim. Then to fix a bolt on the float. This is my favorite kind of job. I mean it needed just a bit more of strength and coordination than I believed I possessed. This time it was a two wrench job—one arm under the float, one over, with me lying flat on my belly while northwesterly wind slapped water all over me. It ended with success.

All the clan except the little Ernies [113] are up and last night all were over. Mike borrows big ladder to fix his laundry yard fence; Irving paints some candle sticks, everyone at his constructive life of important trifles.

Sun and gentle weather makes us all contented and less critical of life, each other, and most important, of our own selves.

So Joan invites us for supper and then plane to La Guardia.

Monday, June 20

My law days—clients are so different from my friends on Main Street. E. S. and Herb for lunch—both in a hurry. Dinner at Plaza with the Lords. Heard championship fight on radio and still not tempted to want to witness one of those outlets for sadism.

[112] Dr. Stephen Gumport.
[113] The Roger Ernsts.

Tuesday, June 21

Dinner with Mr. and Mrs. Alfred Hart, he editor of Macmillan and she discerning daughter of Dave Lawrence. Sterling Lord set up the dinner and we discussed my hunch about a new kind of law book for laymen: no Latin, no mystery, no emphasis on what the press deems to be most of law—rape and murder. I enjoyed showing off by trying out a wide variety of ideas.

Noted that Nixon proposes my Nehru plan for world food surpluses be handled by United Nations. What an odd political situation—Adlai and Nelson, most attractive of candidates for millions in both parties, play cute—of course they are not candidates; of course their best friends say publicly that they are. Something lacking in dignity about playing coy with the leading job in our nation.

Wednesday, June 22

Good weather. Office busy, but the human race starts to look human. What a difference a few week ends, and a spot of sun will make. Andrew L.[114] for lunch—a pleasant able man who knows how to live. Dinner with Edna and we swapped impressions on the hopelessness of our nation if TV and the daily press are allowed to continue to corrupt the taste and standards of our people toward sadisms and cruelties.

Against sleep for some reason, so to books. Shocked to learn that incest is by no means a universal taboo. I knew of the success of Ptolemies in their pro-incest centuries of power, but now I note that whereas some tribes include

[114] Andrew Loebl, old friend.

141

marriages of second cousins within incest taboo, in Indo-china among certain tribes brother and sister may mate provided, and this is a neat proviso, they have not been brought up together.

Thursday, June 23

Up early for plane to Nantucket. Slept badly since I didn't trust the alarm set for 6:15 A.M. Then slept through the call—my own unconscious resisting the clock; up at 6:30, dressed and to La Guardia in plenty of time. There's Maggie at the airport. Dozens of intimate items to be passed between us. The garden is out—not all the roses, but those on Connie's childhood room are lusher than ever.

Read without interruption except for a swim, *Felix Frankfurter Reminisces* by Phillips [115] of Columbia. Enjoyed it all immensely. I do so agree with his admiration for the British who write rather than telephone for appointments. The phone is, I agree, an instrument of invasion of one's privacy. And so I say to Maggie no wonder the British mail is so far superior to U.S. mail. In England it is the prime first choice of all gracious communication. I don't remember being called up for a date in England; that blue letter-paper shows up.

Great letters from Roger in India.

Saturday, June 25

Gloomy, overcast weather and by evening the government weather broadcast indicated a possible tornado over lower

[115] Dr. Harlan Phillips.

N.H. and Vt.—with hailstones on the way up from Penna. The Cape and Islands are outside the path, but the barometer is dropping fast, so will watch our weather instruments. I still want one instrument that records all the factors: tide, moon, temperature, humidity, barometer, wind speed and direction, rainfall, and so forth. To see those curves together written with contemporaneous pens might show correlations pointing to short-term predictions—or at least recurrences.

Helped Mike put together a Sears bureau—with printed instructions better than usual, but of course a few screws and nails were missing. It serves people right. They should make their own. Certainly we should in our power-equipped shop.

Reread Roger's formidable and informative letters from Delhi. Bought and regret Coale-Hoover book entitled *Population Growth and Economic Development in Low Income Countries*. What a fraudulent title, since it is mainly India and a dip into Mexico. A more honest title would have included something like "In Two Low Income Nations." I don't say it's not a good job for specialists in those two lands, but I was sucked in by my friends at Princeton University Press. I think I'll do a volume *Wealth in U.S. Colleges*, and include only Princeton and Williams.

Sunday, June 26

Spent time sailing, swimming and, to get out of sun for brief intervals, opened a book or two. Having no family tradition—not even a family Bible—having not the least information even on great grandparents on either stem of the family, I wish I had kept, as did Judge Holmes, a list of my book readings over the past fifty or sixty years. Just the year and the titles and authors. At least I would have a chance of giving proper answer when asked, "What books affected you deeply?"

Spent a few minutes of great pleasure making a new side for a hot toast-muffin box which Grace and Bennett [116] gave us thirty years ago and which we have used every day every summer since. One side warped—so to my electric saw, matched a piece of wood and did the necessary nailing, staining, and so forth. A job done is a pleasure.

Monday, June 27

Yesterday finished reading *Legacy of Suppression* by Leonard Levy. I enjoyed it in part because it documents what I have long believed: The Founding Fathers, including Jefferson, did not believe in freedom of speech or press without limit. The framers did not once mention freedom of the mind in the four months of debate in 1787 in Philadelphia. And the First Amendment was derived from a fear that the National Congress might cut into the power of the states and abridge speech and press. Content they were to let the states pull out their blue pencils as each saw fit. And they saw fit aplenty until 1925, when for the first time, in the Gitlow case, the High Court held that the Fourteenth Amendment to the Constitution was meant to bring the states under the mandate forbidding censorship of speech and press.

Levy overlooks the real revolution when Holmes and Brandeis laid the emphasis of freedom, not on the speaker or the printer, but on the right of all of us to read, to see,

[116] Epstein, old friends.

to hear. This shift of emphasis to the market place could not make sense until we developed literacy and communication. So don't try it in Africa or South America or India where these two tools are absent.

The garden is adult and adventurous, and we both say we must be a trifle mad to leave this beauty spot for joys and hardships of cruising in Maine.

Tuesday, Wednesday, Thursday, June 28, 29, 30

Start of a new life—a different if not new. Plane to Boston, usual mix-up on airplane tickets; lunch at airport—boiling masses of people in and out. What revolution will occur in near future when the average per capita air use is doubled! Every airport will be inadequate. At Bangor, cab to Farnham Butler's Yacht Yard. There saw my chartered ship sails all out ready for a shake-down with Alan and Paula aboard with Farnham. Stowed our duffel and said goodbye to a nervous owner who wants me as a charterer but hates to see his love in my hands—in fact, in any hands other than his own. I know how I felt when I let others take over my Episode—and I have little of that property sense enjoyed or suffered by others.

Chugged in a hot sun down to Northeast—Maggie's favorite harbor. To town—empty—for a little meal and back to comfortable well-designed Constellation. Hoisted my own burgee—turned in early, all of us under insufficient blankets, not having located the four extra blankets stowed forward. Alan and Paula chose a small but separate cabin far aft— so we stayed in luxury in the largest and most gracious cabin on any 36-foot yawl afloat.

During the next days we were getting acquainted—just finding out if we want to go steady. All important parts of a boat have peculiarities, the alcohol stove—so different from our gas one—the folding table, the location of tools and table ware. They must quickly be assimilated—so that everyone puts everything back in the same spot in the same cuddy every time. Especially is this true on deck, binoculars, Lloyds Register, charts and all those instruments that really run our lives.

Fog in and out on Wednesday so though we started East for Roque Island we heard the government weather report at 12:20 and put back to N.E. Few cruising boats—only two in fact. Then Wednesday off again and one of those days of successive events. Pea soup fog and still we hit our Western Way gong on the nose, and heard and came right on to Bass Head Lighthouse. Fog so thick that we turned sharp to the north and hugged the eastern shore of Bass Harbor.

Most restful and the more it's restful, the more sleep I need and the more I take. No one thinks of anything. Minds are not much needed; the office, the city, the world have disappeared. All our decisions and talk and contemplations are about trivia—mostly weather, and tide, and current, and keeping warm and fed. The stove is on gimbals and has a naughty tilt while we light it—this takes more of our attention than the reality of Castro and Russia, married and threatening our liberty. So we read and discuss for random minutes, the plots of unwritten novels. Haven't handled sails enough to get in sympathy with the boat—but being a lazy, casual cruising person I resent the double sheeted jib, and if I buy the boat will put it on a boom even though I lose seventy feet of sail area and some little amount of speed. There is nowhere I have to go, nowhere I want to be. Each harbor has its beloved recollections. As I write we recall that we anchored right here—near Spar 5—last year and went to visit Alan Klotz, ex-President of the Bar Association of New York City. So many presidents of the Bar Association sail boats, that it is hard to explain why its conglomerate impact on New York is so stuffy. Maggie reports: can't even see the shore fifty yards away.

July

Friday and Saturday, July 1 and 2

Each day is different, but together they are indistinguishable. This has no similarity to the Caribbean where the weather every day is the same. For here we have had a little of all kinds of weather each day—fog in early morning or fog rolling in after four or five o'clock. A bit of mild wind and spots of good sailing winds. It's not easy to recall the name of the harbor in which we dropped a hook or picked up a friendly mooring.

It's a good livable boat we chartered. It's as carefully found as one would expect if one knew its Harvard-Maine Coast owner.

So we talk little to each other; read practically nothing—although I just finished Hough's *Lament for a City*, listen to no radio except weather reports—and spend our sixteen waking hours doing nothing, just lots of nothings.

Feel too healthy, although for the first few days it occurred to me that age was catching up with me, for not until today did I go for a prebreakfast swim, or rather dip, in the cold waters off the Maine Coast.

Sunday, July 3

This was a day unique. I am proud to have met it, and hope never to meet another like it. We were comfortable in North Haven, fast to a sturdy guest mooring. Despite conflicting and changing weather forecasts, we woke up in a pea soup fog, with estimates of wind up to 40 mph in gusts, with fog to recede and return by evening with squalls and rains. So to shore for a stroll. Watched lads on bicycles trailing homemade wooden airplanes—which never did rise from the road no matter what the speed of the cyclist. At about eleven four boats with bare masts chugged by to the western side of this popular water thoroughfare. So off we went, despite the small craft warning pennants. We aimed only for Pulpit, Tom Lamont's hospitable and squall-proof harbor —guarded for three hundred years by the osprey nest on the pulpit-shaped rock. By the time we got to Fiddler Ledge high granite beacon, we could not see as far as the red beacon on Drunkard Ledge. That was the moment when Maggie and I at least would have turned back, but somehow we all (for at least *I* am controlled by what others think or might think) decided to go on. Of course there was no moment of decision. As one does during most of life, I skidded by that special second. On we went with helpful jigger and jib in this sweet dry vessel. I laid a course to keep off a bending shore—with indentations often so gradual that the turns into Wooster and other coves could not be discerned even if seen. But we saw nothing. Blind sailing—hoping that the fog might lift enough to spot some landmarks such as the "largest" (word on the chart) chimney north of Wooster Cove. We saw nothing—scarcely the bow of our boat from the stern. I put out the taffrail log and decided not to make for Pulpit, about two miles to the northeast and right along the shore. There was no chance of finding that narrow entrance unless we could sight it fifty yards away—and the rocks off shore made it too risky. So, risk for risk, I charted a course across to dirty, noisy, but wide-stretched-out Rockland Harbor. I kept going on a mixture of mysticism and pragmatism. On the chart itself we drew the line, marked out each mile, wrote the exact minute when the log clocked a mile. We compared it with estimates of speed on our Kenyon. Alan at the wheel stuck firmly to 270°. Paula and Maggie handled the foghorn every few minutes with a blast. All was tense—the shore we aimed at was not without dangers. I experienced fright—a rare bit of life for me, physically or emotionally. Even thought—as Maggie later told me she had also—that if we could not spot the breakwater, or the Samoset tank, or hear the horn or the siren to guide us in, we would sail up and down in open water until the fog lifted in the morning. Not a pleasant idea. But with a bit of luck when the fog thinned out a trifle, we saw the headland, the tank and the breakwater. Rockland became a loved one. On the way in from the harbor lighthouse we got friendly advice from fishermen on their boats, picked up a heavy mooring, and quietly looked at each other with relief and mutually congratulatory eyes. Lunch and then Alan and Paula aft to their cabin to sleep. Maggie and I too excited. Sleep lives on more than utter physical weariness. It requires a kind of surcease of mind.

Wind keeps up but contentment rules our waves. This

was one of those bits of life—worth living, I suppose, maybe good for reminiscing, but never, I trust, to be relived. Like my trip to Europe on a cattleboat when I was eighteen, or the time I walked across Vermont with blisters on my feet, in pain and—stupidly or wisely—refusing to take a hitch.

Monday, July 4

Left Rockland with smooth sea and off to Pulpit Harbor, one of the best, I'm sure, in the world. Protected and maintained by its owners with the kind of dignity and care that goes with second and third generation wealth. New riches are immature—and so often tactless. Note Wall Street capital gains boys and note Hollywood silver screen girls. Their insecurities drive them to gaudy display in homes, and gardens, and vacation choices. Dropped the hook and hailed Tom [117] sailing his small, life-belted grandson Douglas, and then Tom's daughter and attractive, city planner fiancé come aboard—to solve the world in an hour, a practice we have pursued with Tom for many years. Then Maggie heard a voice not heard for at least a year—it was Steb Bowles [118] rowing out with attractive youngsters aboard.

Then off to Camden, for tomorrow we change crews.

An embarrassment of no little dimension. I ran the boat into minor trouble—scraping the underwater rails of Peterson's shipyard. No great problem but we worried because it was not our own boat. Up to town for dinner. All places but one were closed and that one was stuffy and hot; but found a pleasant, vivacious waitress who made up for badly cooked steak.

It's been a great week—tough going, tense, relaxed, hot,

[117] Thomas Lamont of Morgan Guaranty Trust Co.
[118] Mrs. Chester Bowles.

cold. No lack of variation in nature's tricks noted on the sea —seldom in the city. To find a buoy is more important than what Mr. K. says to Mr. E.

From Tuesday, July 5 to Sunday, July 10

I sent previous diary notes to Paula to type up, so I don't know when I last made my random jottings. Maybe I did mention Camden with its pleasant club and people and its unpleasant roll. On one day recently—how irrelevant time becomes—Alan and Paula deserted our after cabin for a plane to New York and then to Europe for vacation for three weeks. Good crew and in truth the mood of cruising, so unlike anything else on land or sea, had gotten them so, that with a good sailboat for three weeks, they might have cancelled their flight to Paris. Alan and I did quite some work—but that is not the name for stretching of minds on matters legal —on libel, estate matters, taxation of authors and second basemen, and the U.S. Supreme Court brief in Birth Control case.

Then Gordon[119] and Paul[120] came on as crew. Both greener than good for a boat on blue water. Anxious to learn —but teaching in variable weathers is not easy. They didn't even know the vernacular. As I write I look up to the cockpit and see Maggie in her mail-order-from-Seattle blue hunting dress—with hands on the wheel and legs astride. Unconventional for a Natchez maid.

Left Camden after picking up mail left at the club—one of the two clubs where I was asked to withdraw my name. Here Curtis Bok[121] suggested I join and then found embarrass-

[119] Gordon Rogoff.
[120] Paul Viera, actor from South Africa.
[121] Late author, jurist of Philadelphia and Camden.

153

ment. This on grounds of so-called race—what's wrong with my kind of Aryanism? At Century in New York, Loomis [122] —a rock of the club—with support of Murrow, Gunther and others, could not get me by. I was told they were blocked by a lawyer of import—a seeming friend—about whom I have no doubt spoken words to show I want a very different world than he does. Or, in fact, he may have had more valid objections.

To Pulpit Harbor again where Tom, his daughter, fiancé and grandchild came aboard, and later Maggie and I walk up for coffee after dinner. Gave Elinor Lamont a copy of *Touch Wood*, after rereading what I said about these easy-to-meet people of culture when last in Pulpit. Tom gave me a copy of letters written by his son Tom, who died at twenty-one on the submarine Snook during the war. This slender privately-printed volume has done something to me. I never have read of or met this type of lad before. He was in love with North Haven as our Roger loves our island. He was an explorer—of flora and fauna—and talks of the osprey as if they were of his kith and kin. His growth away from his pro-Socialist Uncle Corliss, showed remarkable precognition of where Russia would go after the war. His comments on the waste of human life in the Navy—not by death but by living boredom—should be read by the Secretary of Defense today. I now know dead Tom—maybe better than I do his living father—and could weep for his death. Tom of today seems to be midway between old Tom, his father, of the Parsonage book, and this dead son.

From Pulpit to Alan Norton's shipyard in Gilkey Harbor where a good workman replaced the Kenyon fin. I recall when Rog and I first did such a job on Episode. That hole of two-inch diameter and the gush of water from the sea was frightening, but a hole of small dimensions is no such peril

[122] Loomis Harmon, architect and Nantucket neighbor.

as is a leaky seam. When done, the mechanic said, "Is two dollars O.K.?" No abuse of foreigners up here. We should have Fulbright exchange workmen from big cities to the villages of our great Republic.

Then a great sail for Castine—which we approached under skies black with peril, rain and high winds. No mooring available and so happily we were directed to a cove across the Bagaduce river to lie with about thirty cruising boats from Eastern Yacht Club of Marblehead, Massachusetts. Gay and handsome as skies cleared up, and later full moon gave us a glare. To shore for provisions and called up Polly and Molly [123] who have lived here—leaving Castine only five times in three years. At dinner at their nongustatory club we had another glimpse at gallant age. Molly is eighty-six, drives to Boston, ran for state senate; and Polly, a decade younger, looks less than sixty. When I asked if she had a fortune of dollars what she would buy, she had only two ideas: rebuild the bay window of their house facing the Penobscot on snug Perkins' Cove, and clean out the underbrush in their pines. Molly, when talking to Paul about his insoluble native land, South Africa, said, "I'm too old to be interested in one more continent. Nothing of significance can happen there in my remaining years."

And so memories on ship continue to merge as they seldom do on land. Morning, noon, night are all part of a whole— and the only purpose of time is the reckoning distance gone or to be gone on a foggy day or to be sure we make a harbor before sundown.

How many days—that is, calendar days—have I dreamed through without markers sufficient to identify a day in a diary. I'll check up later—or maybe never be curious enough to check.

[123] Miss Polly Porter and Miss Mary W. Dewson.

Maggie explains the weedy muck and wood that covers the waters. This is the week of unusual high tide—two feet above normal in this area, and hence the muck off the rocky shores has been detached and taken to sea. Just so does much of man's muck get into circulation when international high tides unloose passions and action out of desperate ignorance. So now at last the muck encouraged by Herbert Matthews of the *Times* gives the White House navigation troubles around Cuba. Sixteen days after Castro got into Havana I predicted at Morgan's, at lunch, that Cuba would go to Khrushchev and that Matthews would—as he did—encourage (out of the same unwitting confusions he displayed in the Spanish War) and favor (by predicting and not seeing the danger of Communism ninety miles from Florida) the wiping out of the middle class in Cuba. Some day I may publish my letters of warning, written a year ago to Morse, Fulbright and Dick Nixon. We are in trouble—far different and more telling than in the Near East. What the hell. The Deer Island bridge is ahead. I'll look at beauty; I'm in favor of escape—a locale good for running to, but evil if the impetus is for running away.

From Castine we sailed through Eggemoggin Reach and as usual had to tack, despite the local myth that one always had a fair wind and a good reach down this stretch of water. I shall not be hard on local legends—for surely I would prefer local to international knowledge. The latter is so vast that it becomes little more than a parlor toy, save for those who are near seats of power where knowledge can be used. Local knowledge on the other hand is potent, and man can and must act thereon.

On to Center Harbor; Stablefords not up in their rambling white house this summer. Dropped the hook in the cove of Chatto Island, the boys swam to the island and fetched back mammoth mussels—I recalled Roger bringing back two bucketsful at Jewel Island, Casco Bay, probably twenty-five years ago.

Ate well—lobster and wine for lunch, and steak for dinner. Good to lie in a stout but subsiding wind. The next day must have been Sunday, the 10th, for the radio was blocked up with pontifical voices—the kind no one uses for speech except in sermons. Gentle but overcast, so down Leadbetter Reach to Lareys and then, instead of going out to Penobscot, we turned around and doubled back on this reach, which Maggie prefers to all others. Sailed on—with winds defying predictions of U.S. Weather Bureau—into Camden for change of crews. Much business to be done: mend a small tear in mizzen sail; water; gas.

Maggie will leave and I'm not happy. But two weeks is all the discomfort she prefers—with her bed and garden urging her back to Nantucket.

Monday, July 11

The day is a Monday in July. Maggie has sidled off ship for her roses in Nantucket. Here I am for a night on shore— and partly because Maggie would be much happier than if I had stayed alone on the Constellation. Somehow she thinks because I have nearly finished seventy-two years that I'm getting older.

This expensive and luxurious hostelry, the Samoset, has everything that money—and it takes a real hunk of money— can buy. A Hotel it is—in no sense an Inn. Both have porches with rocking chairs but I'll wager the chairs at this big hotel are wider—or need to be wider—than at a smallish, sensible inn, such as Hastings runs at Somes House. The behinds of women are wider in big hotels.

So I'm on my own after days of minor challenges. Why

does man concern himself, in talk at least, with the big challenge? I read about the greatest issue of the campaign, the most important international problem that faces man. I guess we enjoy the giant queries because they are insoluble and hence anyone can disagree with the author—for the author is only guessing too. On ship there are few, if any, big enemies, but a constant dance with little ones every minute of the day—a halyard tugged up the last inch, the sheet let out a trifle, the choice of knot in a piece of rope.

So I'm here among a special sector of mankind—rich, but mostly from that hard-working, ambitious, generous and utterly insecure group. So I go back to an earth rhythm. Why were Winthrop Aldrich and his bride so friendly to us at the airport and so frank about his concern over Cuba and the lack of organized concentration at the White House? Will the report of Norman St. John Stevas—a British R.C.— on the lack of morality of the Church position on contraception influence my friends who have failed to appreciate the mobility and viability of the Church of Rome? Why does *Herald Tribune* carry such stories on front page, whereas the great *Times*—our greatest paper—hides such reports? Why was I so ineffective during the past year when I wrote, urged, talked on radio and wherever people would listen to me, about the take-over of Cuba by Russia? This is the great debacle of our nation. And so I read the daily papers, take a hot bath, get a haircut, and try unsuccessfully to get in with waiters and waitresses—college kids and from all over the United States. I can't make the grade. I'm too old, too well off—in fact, in the employer class. So I look out on the Rockland breakwater and wait for tomorrow when the Bessie gang make my new and last crew of the summer.

Tuesday, July 12

Several hot baths, shave with running hot water. Effete life —when heated H_2O takes on such significance. Only the other day when a few were asking, "In what past period would you care to have lived?" I said I didn't think I could have taken Florence in the Medici era—but for the age of the 1787 Founding Fathers I'd give up hot water and other conveniences.

Watched TV Democratic Convention, without fire or sense of urgency. The keynote speech was good for ordinary days and ordinary conventions but what we needed was statesmanship—difficult these days when the entire drive of the press and TV is for fights, bad news, trouble.

Could not get Tommy Lamont and "book" out of my mind. Three hundred privately-printed copies not enough. This was a rare lad.

New crew gets off Nantucket and arrives in Rockland early afternoon where I surprise them at the airport—and then back to the boat and my other world.

The help—all colleges types—at the hotel have more fun than the guests. One attractive lad from Kansas is just crazy about English which he will teach. "What period of English authoring do you prefer?" "Oh, Mr. Ernst, you don't understand. I'm an expert on grammar. I love grammar." This I thought is like the lawyer who adores Demurrers.

Read both *Harper's* and *Atlantic*. The latter issue is more to my liking, what with wise Judge Bazelon writing about the inane drive for punishment, and Bowen's [124] delicious article on Harold Ober—the most helpful authors' representative I ever knew.

[124] Katherine Drinker Bowen.

Wednesday, July 13

Restless slumbers. Our vessel fell in love with the giant mooring post and in a windless night kept seeking it out. They bumped each other with no violence, but it was disturbing enough that three or four times I had to go above, give them a good talking to and separate them as best I could with the pole.

With a fair tide went out, picking our way from island to island, having taught Nick how to chart a course. I'm getting old. Old enough to be disappointed when youngsters do not measure up to Roger's early curiosity, coordination and deftness on a sailboat. Most other kids although agile, are too goddamn verbal and I guess, although I'm quite a chatterer on law, on a boat I utter little of what I think and nothing of what I feel.

Good news from office and mail from friends, all brought up by Mike. It was thoughtful of Maury and Bill [125] to telephone me yesterday. Just friendly intercourse—little purpose other than friendliness, and what better?

Tonight we listened to Democratic convention, while I, like a dog worrying a bone, keep our national dilemmas circling in my mind—being quite sure that the matrix of our sorry state is due to the fact that Ike does not read reports, and so all under him are seldom kept on their toes. If he only made believe he read reports, then all would become mentally active again. In the State Department the old heads under Foster were, it seems, corrupted beyond repair, corrupted by a total loss of adventure, ingenuity, or a sense of constant urgency. Our foreign office is a mess, never having gotten away from Dulles' headlines to the sober arts of diplomacy.

[125] Maurice Greenbaum and William Wolff, law partners.

So, as Connie said, why should we not expect the Gallupized-Madison Avenue-mass media to flow from sales of beer and cosmetics into the realm of politics. So Kennedy is nominated—really no debate, no deliberation, no stubborn group, even, of obstinate men. So all climb the wagon, afraid —in the power game of politics—to prefer conviction to the comfort of being on the side of the winner. I'd bet a couple of petty vice-presidents that, on a secret ballot, the result would have been quite different. I'm not at all happy about this type of monied maneuver to select presidential candidates—no more than I like the Nixon succession theory which has developed in the Republican party. Maybe in a country as large as ours, it will be difficult to invent anything better until we have, as President Taft urged, cabinet members converted to responsibility by the adoption of the British system of party responsibility.

From Bucks, we left with good U.S. Weather Bureau cheer: clearing by noon. By noon, off Torrey's, it started to rain— and pour it did. Finally we found our tired, cold way into Burnt Coat Harbor on Swan's Island. I lit Tiny Tot; we had hot Bovril and then relaxed and waited for a banquet ending with a bottle of Pouilly Fuissé and crepes suzette. Tired, and to the so-called hay. Although it blew hard, the anchor, a good twenty-pound plow, held well. And so we hear the undemocratically-arrived-at arrangement for Johnson to be Vice-President. I suggest that Kennedy will find his first embarrassment when dealing with heads of states in South America where church and state are substantially identical. However, Johnson, older, and wiser, will not find it easy to be an errand boy and clerk, and this will be good for the White House. The real question is: did Adlai release Schlesinger, Commager, to Kennedy, and, whether by deal or not, will Adlai become Secretary of State? It will be odd for a president to be ambushed by two men like Lyndon and Adlai, men who have power on their own. Compare to any of F.D.R.'s Vice-Presidents or Secretaries of State, all of whom owed selection to F.D.R.—and not to political or popular power.

Friday, July 15

Skies cleared by wind and rain, to shore to see this eighty-school-children (three-teacher) village of Burnt Coat on Swan's Island. Chatted with postmistress, then to grocer and on way back to wharf invited into home of the doctor to play chess. (He has only two playing companions on Swan's Island.) Once he rowed around General Patton's "When and If" and asked if anyone on board would come to shore to play a game with him. A true gentleman accepted the invitation and in addition brought along a bottle of Scotch. This doctor—the only one on the island—practiced for thirty-five years in Bangor and now at eighty must soon be replaced. Not easy. A sign in post office explains that folk are in peril if they get a bellyache from green apples or confinement—both to be avoided.

Prediction: 10-20 winds from N.W. Sure enough it was gentle—off-shore or S.W. and we dawdled, tacking under sail all day between friendly islands until we rounded Merchants and found our way into the northern end of Isle au Haut, just below the island of the O. W. Holmes family on our starboard, and to port we were a short row from the Bowdoin Davis' [126] simple summer home. These Baltimore folk have been casuals in our life, we never having seen either except

[126] Baltimore surgeon.

in Maine at this very spot. They didn't come up until August but loaned their house to bridal couple.

Drinks with them. But that's enough to create acquaintances.

On board I'm floundering in comic books up to my ass. Nick's cousin, a boy of unusual mind, would be good company at a planetarium, library or at any game using words, but he has little interest as yet in the sea. I have failed miserably to excite him even about knots or furling a line. Nick, without him, could be like Rog, but now Nick no longer asks to handle the wheel or chart tomorrow's course on the handsome government charts. He prefers comics. Not easy to get good company for my kind of cruising—maybe there is none without Maggie on board. Those gay boats with a group of men make sense only as floating bars.

Few porpoises and no seal during the past days. But on the rocks the white gulls and the black cormorants take their segregated positions. Even on a small rock they don't seem to integrate; a good yard between the groups is enough to satisfy "separate and equal" facilities.

Saturday, July 16

Cruising is a unique way of life. As special and rare as life in a convent or the existence of deep-sea divers or mountain climbers. In a way it's most unique, if unique can carry a superlative. (Maggie says it can't.) It requires personalities in tune with the blue water and, in addition, the comradeship of sailing companions—one or more, in an intimacy tighter and under strains more severe at times than any family on land. Maggie and I have been unable to find few others—outside of our very own intimate family—with whom the intimacy of life below deck in a room 8 × 24 feet, and

163

the need for alert and often strenuous cooperation on deck, can be lived with mutual respect and be gaily pursued hour after hour. A small boat must have a crew so closely knit as to come close to brushing each other's teeth.

I can stand on board a degree of drunkards or a quantity of *mal de mer*. The one thing I can't bear on board is the person who is and remains phlegmatic, unthrilled by a view, unexcited by the accuracy of a course charted to avoid a hidden rock, or unelated by a sunrise or a sunset. Those who spend most of their time below, those who have no curiosity about the luff of a sail or the annoyance of a slapping halyard or the untidiness of an Irish pennant, should stay ashore— or at least off my vessels and not make believe they enjoy my type of ghosting on a breathless day or the bending of a sail after a bitter, cold and wet attempt to make a harbor.

I can sail single-handed. I can idle in a harbor alone with Maggie; but at my age, for ranging a coast it takes a crew, and crews are rare—too, too rare. No George Allen type of court jester fits. Intellectuals are good—in fact, in demand in our life—but in a library or what used to be called a sitting room.

Off for Blue Hill—another warm day. Winds predicted to perfection, to fit my course, to suit my idea of speed. Blew up to 25 in gusts. Picked up buoy close to a Concordia. Lots of swims. Then to town, shopping, the last of the cruise, and to eat blueberry pancakes.

To pillow early.

Sunday, July 17

To dock of clubhouse early for a little gas, water, ice and to call Maggie. All well at home, and I do miss her. I doubt I'll cruise again without her. I sure miss Roger, who is at his gayest and most relaxed when cruising, but he'll not return from Delhi until 1962.

Ralph Perkins [127] came over to club and we exchanged our uninformed guesses on politics: Nixon's running mate, who will win in November, and so forth. Fantastic the amount of talk in our nation on outcomes of political competitions. The stress is as if the franchise were a guessing game—people conjecture without knowledge or, what is worse, without any strong feelings. The zeal of prophecy seems to flatter our citizenry.

Off in light southerlies and fair sky, looking for a picnic spot where water is not too deep to drop a hook and where a flat, water-smoothed stone will make an entrance into the water delectable.

Good steak, cooked in a cove near Sawyer's. Swim and back to boat with zippy wind which died before we went into the formidable and still friendly Western Way. Saltonstall's handsome sloop chugged by us with the Roman figure of the Senator at the wheel.

Mooring found with ease and only the next day did I learn the Law of Moorings. No one owns a mooring in navigable waters. Even our pier at Monomoy required War Department consent before it could be erected thirty years ago. I lamented with the Senator, who confessed his regret that he could not sail to Chicago for the Republican convention.

Monday, July 18

Gray day. To town. Bought my papers, did double-acrostic with more than my usual passion. Took car to Bangor and plane to New York, leaving Mike and Connie to clean ship

[127] Williams classmate, Cleveland and Georgia industrialist.

and turn her back to Farnham, with whom I had a brief talk of boats. So to New York and my other life—truly other.

Tuesday, July 19

Back in the mammoth horde called New York City. I recall when a child I didn't see the city except on the one day when the family came back from the summer vacation. The elevated railroads, the skyscrapers—six stories high—held my surprised gaze. But even now I see a new city each time I return. Why is there no single tree after I pass 13th Street on Fifth Avenue? At least up to 40th where I turn east? Why did I shift my desires so quickly from the quest for meaning to the search for certainty? Are people so truly different in summer than in winter? Is it deeper than the tan of the sun on faces?

To the office where all is a mess with painters and engineers for air conditioning. I hate the new telephone with its efficient multiple buttons. Yes, I can get people more quickly, but what is the merit of saving seconds or even minutes? In a real sense I think I'd like to go back to 2 Rector Street where the four of us and only one employee, Ethel H.[128]— still with us—started in constant competition with the noisy Sixth Avenue El, which ran by our windows, not more than six feet away.

For lunch with Herb and Herb, Jr. and for dinner with Albert and Nell Boni at Charles, that good restaurant which has the same cashier since it opened as a pastry shop in 1916.

Home early. Watched a ball game on TV, read my favorite science magazines, *New Scientist* and *Science Newsletter,* which raised questions quite remote from the direction of the current in Casco Passage or the Deer Island Thorofare.

[128] Ethel Hirshman.

Another look at the Square, scarcely to be seen through the heavy-leaved trees that touch my little porch.

As I fell asleep I thought of some of the generous, considerate letters that had come in about *Touch Wood*. And just before I went off I recall thinking how I drew out of my drawer my only shirt that requires cuff buttons. For without Maggie, I can't, without great travail, get my hand in or out of a buttoned shirt and have never learned to put the links in after the shirt is on. Important items even for a sleepy mind.

Wednesday, July 20

A day full of events and good surprises and pleasures. For breakfast with Carlisle of Nantucket, editor of Purdy, Carlisle & Dodd, one of the new firms made up of youth, zeal and good will. He wants me to do a book I have tentatively titled "United World Through Humor." I'd get humor, wit, in stories of each nation and then headnote each nation, thus pointing to different attitudes of laughing at oneself and at neighbors. It ought to be easy if I go to the UN and get up a series of luncheons for officials connected with each legation. I'm sure if I say I understand there is no humor in Ethiopia, coupled with a denial, I'll get typical stories. If I can do what I'm after I should get Dag Hammarskjöld or Dave Owen or some top official to do the foreword.

Then at lunch with Bennett Cerf at Sardi's East, enjoying, while waiting, a talk with Papa Sardi. At lunch we took up many of the ills of book publishing. I think I disturbed Bennett when I asked why he permits a tariff on book paper, while newsprint comes in free of any. Discussed my new approach to travel guides—guides to folkways rather than to buildings or paintings or shrines.

For dinner with Harry Horner whose mind I enjoy more at every meeting. Discussed our *How to Make a Man*. Spoke to Sterling Lord who has a contract agreeable to me for a series of twelve law books for Macmillan. They think my approach may be a breakthrough so that the layman will get a better look at the law. Quite different from murder, mayhem and orgy—the tabloid depiction of the court system.

Conference with varied clients; used up three stenographers; tried to use the new, improved, many-buttoned telephone gadget; wrote to R. L. and many in Washington who had written me; answered gracious notes of praise on *Touch Wood* from receivers of prepublication copies. Telephoned Maggie; saw most of partners not galavanting in Europe. Home early and to bed. Turned on TV, tried each station, turned off TV.

Woke up in the middle of the night, about 3 A.M. My thought was why not withdraw all—every single one—of our air bases from foreign lands and announce we will, as we now can, protect peace and our allies for freedom with floating bases—now that we can send missiles 1,000 miles from submarines submerged for a year or more. This may relieve tensions and save billions which we could invest in education of our youth, the best investment of a nation. As I returned to sleep I thought we might be able to trade removal of bases for Russia's agreement to restore freedom to all its colonies, including Latvia and Lithuania—too often forgotten.

Thursday, July 21

Plane to home, garden and Maggie. Met at airport and undressed in car so when I stepped out with my white shorts I told the grandchildren that I had flown up without shirt or shoes. Garden is rife, roses lush and our atomic-bombarded corn is a foot high. Swims, lunch in garden.

Went to look over our compound. The Goldsteins had painted their window-trim Yellow—with a capital "Y." The Bedfords [129] had helped them. Everyone seemed busy, hence happy.

Lots of chores. Ladder on float had a broken holdback, halter on Rainbow had given way, the beach grass from our house demands scythe, two trees need trimming.

So content at work and at sleep and much to ponder. Dr. H.,[130] a pathologist, says cells are identifiable as to sex. Even a cell at the end of my nose? Yes. But are all cells in what we call a male really and fully male? Isn't there a variety of degrees of maleness in cells? So far gradations have not been discovered. I was going to say "or invented." For surely after man has discovered, he can invent a facsimile of nearly everything. Synthetic is the word of the era.

Friday wind blows up to 35 but few clouds and barometer is steady. About a score of beautiful Cruising Club sailboats enter the harbor.

Haagensen tells me of his compound on the Cape. About thirty members of the family, a brick house for grandchildren under twelve—an aged compound, begun before the turn of the century when Mrs. H.'s father and another professor located, by buggy, the spot on their little harbor or cove on the Cape.

In proportion to its use by man, the sea is probably safer than the land. And surely less hazardous than the mountains —not to mention man's madness in hugging Mt. Etna, which, exploding again, shouts with fire in the air: "I've killed a million of you humans in 2,400 years. How many more before you keep away from my door?"

129 George and Jean, New Jersey friends.
130 Cushman Haagensen of Medical Center.

Saturday, July 23

Saw our good friends the Fays,[131] both in good health and usual, which means good, spirits. Save only Sidney's eyes which have given out—no more auto driving and his book of many years' effort must be turned over for completion of the last quarter to someone else. Sidney admits he has been a perfectionist—a dire disease which delayed completion—but also he finds some relief in not having it on his mind any longer.

We heard our story of the week, which makes life sound real and rich and not depressing or newsworthy according to standards of our tabloid press.

One day last week Sarah, well over eighty-five years of age, saw a parakeet on her porch. The bird was at ease and friendly—hopped on Sarah's finger and came in with her to the living room. Naturally she called "Information" at the telephone office to find out who was keeping parakeets. In no time at all the word came back: Mrs. Harry Turner. Gordon Turner showed up with a lad of eight, James Hammond. James had brought his cage and took home his pet. A day or so later young Hammond visited Sarah and gave her a tray and a letter. The tray was, as the lad said, the Reward; and the letter said the return of the parakeet was his very, very best birthday present.

Moral 1. The optimum size of livable town or city is one where you can call up the telephone company and ask "who keeps parakeets?"

Moral 2. Rewards given by the young are admirable and always from the heart.

Wet sail in big blow. With Mike, Nick and Kathie to look at the great sailboats in the harbor. In afternoon to town to

[131] Sidney Fay, former Harvard history professor, author, and his wife.

see Nat Benchley's pictures and talk with folk on the docks. For dinner the Goldies and the Bedfords—a farewell to Irv as his vacation is over.

Those were the so-called happenings but somehow the day rushed by. All I did was fix this or that, saw off a branch, tuck back a rose branch, hang a bird feeder and other little chores —each a pleasure in itself and none for any great purpose.

The Williams family departed and it's not human to have Roger's house with no one using it.

Sunday, July 24

It's too beautiful to go to New York. How many more days and nights will be so clear and clean, and how many will Maggie and I have in good health together? For years I have known the date of my death—April 2, 1968. That will make me nearly eighty. Now this act of faith with which I have lived for fifty or sixty years seems to be evaporating. I may live far beyond it. But whatever the number of days, I must stop compromising and ride life for all it's worth. I want nothing big or mighty. I'm content with a multitude of trivia and a few fast friends and above all, freedom from bores.

Sunday I spent three hours with Nicholas, delving into my treasure box of boat gadgets—shackles, snap hooks, slides, turnbuckles. We talked and of course took dream trips together. He's a sheer joy when I have him all alone.

Joan explained her thesis that cats know she is deaf. Her cat rubs against her if she wants milk or if someone is at the door. But if Steffie—who has hearing—is around, the cat uses voice and her limited vocabulary of meows.

To Boat House for dinner for the jumbo shrimp, then to Main Street to listen to the town amateur band, then to pick

up Joan and Steffie at the boat—they having gone for the day
to visit Woods Hole.

Monday, July 25

Lots of reading, but mostly about the Right to Be Let
Alone, more stylishly called the Right to Privacy—a right put
into legal use by L. D. B.[132] through an article in the Harvard
Law Review of 1890. I do suspect that he and Warren, who
wrote the piece, were inspired by Godkin's book which came
out six months earlier.

I'm getting saturated with this clash between privacy and
the needs of history—the joy of privacy and the ease with
which men of good works forego anonymity. An author who
sends a book out for review, a man running for office, an
inventor—in fact any public doer—sacrifices privacy and, by
his very contributions to society, creates a valid public interest in his "personality." But should the peephole columnists
have the right to write about the home, marital and sex life
of a singer? Why should not mention be limited to the singing, the performance? Or does the art of song require for its
growth complete knowledge of all the intimacies of every
songbird? Da Vinci was a bastard, as were also Hamilton
and Ramsay MacDonald. Value in such knowledge? If so,
during the life of the person or only afterwards? Can history
be written at a later date? Many good questions—a game better than my double-crostics.

Tuesday, July 26

Last night to the crowded Unitarian church to hear the
Beaux Arts Trio—a Hadyn that was only ear deep for me,

[132] Justice Louis D. Brandeis.

a Ravel that hit the gonads and a Mendelssohn that aimed at my heart. The audience was mostly grey on top and feminine. Chatted with the philosopher-basket weaver Reyes, whose two sons went from this island to Williams College, and arranged a joint family party for August.

The church, with its forty-foot ceiling and inside shutters for thirty-foot windows is one of my favorites, maybe in part because it was on that platform that I won the case of U.S. *v.* One copy of Joyce's *Ulysses*. When the literary jurist Woolsey asked me twenty-five years ago, "Did you really read the book from cover to cover?" I knew he was saying, "If few people can read it through, why not suppress it?" So I had my answer ready and told Woolsey in effect that when the volume first appeared I tried and couldn't make it out. But later I had to read it in preparation for the trial, and while reading it I was asked to speak on the Bank system and Federal Reserve at the Unitarian Church in Nantucket. The kindly, worried judge rapped on his bench and said, "What's that got to do with my question?" Unpertubed, I continued, "Well, Judge, while talking in that church I thought I was talking only about banks, but when I sat down I recalled that while talking about banks I was, at the same time, thinking about the church clock in the back, the tall windows, the grey-haired women in the front row and hundreds of other items." And then I said, "Judge, I understood Ulysses for the first time. The secondary stream of the mind clarified the writings of Joyce." And I continued, "And now, Judge, while talking about *Ulysses*—anxious to win this cause—I must confess I have, while arguing, been thinking of your gown slipping off your left shoulder, the gold ring around your tie and the picture of Washington hung behind you."

Whereupon the Judge interrupted me to say, "I want to thank you, Mr. Ernst. I'm worried about this case, especially the last fifty pages, but now I comprehend the significance of this volume, for while listening to you as intently as I know how, I'll confess I've also at the same time been thinking about the Heppelwhite chair behind you."

I gave him a victor's smile and said that the book—the dual streams of consciousness—did the same. And then for about ten minutes we discussed the Judge's passion for collecting antiques.

So during the concert my mind went to my friend Woolsey, my talks with Joyce in Paris and the rare occasions when lawyers can act out their causes in the presence of the judge.

Maggie agog for hours. A family of Eastern King Birds lighted on our locust tree—three babies waiting on parents' instructions on a top bough until food was foraged. This and the Fays for lunch were the high spots.

What a spell of weather—one day more beautiful than the other. Soon people will become bored and hope for a little fog or a big blow.

Wednesday, July 27

Publishers' Weekly announced Brut Ehrman's [133] revised book on the Sacco-Venzetti case and mentions that it includes material I gave to Herbert about the true guilty person, Joe Morelli, and my correspondence with him. Society, if once committed, hates to find the truth if it conflicts with previous theories; and in fact many do not want the truth. There are even some who prefer not to find the truth as it may create some degree of absolution for the governor of Massachusetts and the administrator of justice. A philosophy of life I never could understand. Not remote from many liberals who really cannot get themselves to enjoy victories.

Good sail to our favorite deep-water beach where Maggie,

[133] Herbert Ehrman, Boston lawyer.

Connie, Nicholas and I went for a swim. Nick has swimming licked. He's over the hump of confidence, which rather than muscle or wind or technique of arm and leg keeps people on top of the water. It's an important moment as is the capture of every new challenge in life.

Thursday, July 28

Mixed news from my other life—the office. Herb called with distressing information that fell into his lap about a person for whom we have a great concern; Bill W. telephoned about one of his many miracle results in dealing with administrative agencies.

Macmillan offer of contract for three books on law arrived; letter from Alan and Paula who love England as we do.

Here I swam; cut grass; wove a doormat with Steffie out of old rope on my special new machine; made a new floor board for the catboat; and so it went—or I went—from one chore to another.

Maggie woke up to tell me she was resting comfortably in her home in Natchez. She and many others, but not I, remember every detail of every dream. Today she recaptured her desk of sixty years ago—one of those slanted, brown, lid-rising, footboard-underneath pieces—also her bookcase with her special section of poetry. I remember none of my rooms, furniture, or even where I lived at different periods, or with whom I shared a room. We both read and were impressed by Alice Freeman Palmer's life. This was the first of the great women's autobiographies of our younger days. But Maggie's youth and education, particularly from one teacher, gave the book significance as well as pleasure. Mrs. Palmer wrote that when young, she would open one of her books of poetry at random with closed eyes, and whatever poem appeared, she would memorize that day. And so Maggie played that precious game. With what I had, I couldn't participate in that grand style. And now I wonder how many girls or boys would do so today. Is there one in Natchez—or in New York? TV has made a far different world for all of us, particularly the young. Far less participation, far less doing, much more watching.

Saw Republican convention on TV at Fran and Jannine's.[134] I guess exchange of thought in conventions of hundreds, with galleries, with organized whoop-la, and with everyone talking to TV audiences may have some value; but certainly there is lost, probably forever, the process of attempting to change the minds of delegates.

For dinner with Joan and Steffie to the Skipper, and Stef asked one great question. She saw a gull on a roof and asked how it can stand up on the ridge. Good because standing is an easy assumption, and the challenge of all that is said or assumed is valued. So we explained the three toes, the webs between, and illustrated with a table fork on the back of a chair. I wish all people would refuse to accept all knowledge handed on or out. I enjoy a child's inquiry about the usual more than a Hadyn trio, and I don't mean querulous "whys" about going to bed. There's a vast gap between "Why must I go to bed?" and "Why do I need sleep?"

Friday, July 29

Next week in office looks like an active and exciting time. Clients with need for affirmative legal help—if I could only write on such matters. Of course they will never belong to me (but to the client) no matter how dramatic and thrilling the problems may be. Maybe the proper sealing of a lawyer's lips contributes to the confusion and ignorance of the public as

[134] Dr. Frances Arkin, analyst, and Mrs. Jannine Rolland.

to the function of a member of the bar. Our public knows law only as dirtied up by the press, garbled by even the better papers, or out of what each person deems a unique experience when he needs interpretation of any law—even a parking regulation. People have little chance to learn about philosophies underlying the writing of statutes or the rendering of court opinions.

About time I reported to my other gull stations. This year I'm back to hanging dead gulls on the pier, with odd results—quite different from what I understand takes place in Milford, Connecticut, at the Stanford [135] station. I have two dead gulls at end of pier, none on land side. No gulls have sat on rail or fished off land end of pier. At the water end the two dead gulls have had an odd effect. No gulls sit there, but there is some fishing, although only late in evening or at dawn and at most by not more than three or four. Each morning I pick up the empty shells. No great nuisance, but why not fishing all along my pier as there was a few years ago? Surely Nantucket gull population is on the increase.

Muggy weather, but planes have been running on time, even during week ends. Not like last season.

Saturday, July 30

I'm not very old, but on the verge, no doubt, because I welcome proof of nonagedness. Cut grass at Bessies' and the Little Ernies'—big sweat and enjoyed dripping as I have all my life.

Letters came in on *Touch Wood* from Ben Sonnenberg,[136] from whom I haven't heard in years, and from book store

---

[135] Alfred Stanford, yachtsman, editor of Milford *Citizen*.
[136] Public Relations counsel.

owners and even Al Hart and Mrs. Hart, of Macmillan. All most generous.

Good news. A State Department change of head of Caribbean division. Maybe Matthews' policy of letting the revolution in Cuba "run its course until the middle class is wiped out" will be repudiated at long last. In a way I regret we did not agree to represent the Cuban Sugar Institute under Castro, when so invited during the first month he was dictator. We might have done a job on literacy, health and housing through the Institute.

I've been telling many people Rubottom must be let out of control of Cuban affairs in Washington, and now that he is kicked upstairs, some of my friends truly believe that I had received an inside tip. Not so.

Elements run our lives. At near midnight a no-visibility fog came this way. So our ferry, as we heard on short wave radio, ran onto the easterly jetty, backed off to the bell, started to take in water, 140 passengers aboard. Coast Guard was called, and, according to report, nothing was carried on with efficiency. To sleep at 3 A.M. after alerting Mary H., our ham radio expert, who rushed down to help and called us back that all people were safe. One more steamship line escapade and this island will have "had" it, what with the long strike, big deficit and one boat on the rocks in the Hole.

And today "Brenda" is announced to visit us in the late afternoon. Not a hurricane, but the two gale flags are up across the harbor. I guess she will hit here as she does elsewhere at high tide, about 6 P.M. So we battened down, closed garage doors which don't like to be shut. Put tree supports on the locust, closed windows and doors in play house, rowed out to catboat, took in duffel—and took these many precautionary steps for reasons quite complex. To save from damage, yes; but more important, to prove to ourselves that we are wise, farsighted and can stand up to nature.

As to Rubottom, I may be a little cruel. The fault may be Allen Dulles and the CIA. Maybe they minimized two years ago, the Communist plan to infiltrate Cuba, Panama and Venezuela. I suspect the CIA must be inept and probably corrupt, since Dulles reports to no one in any real sense, hence a Rubottom must take the full rap because he may not say, "Why didn't Dulles tell us the facts so that we could abandon our pussy-footed policy for one of unashamed dignity, such as befits our Republic?"

Everyone is exhilarated. The wind is piling up. Rebuttable peril is at hand. Enough danger to be alert and use energy and ingenuity, but not enough to give anyone a sense of inevitable surrender to nature in one of its flare-ups against man's perversions or distortions of natural forces.

Sunday, July 31

No storms ever match the storms (or other perils) of olden times. This only means that the excitements of a hurricane or blizzard when we are young cause forceful memories and destroy man's ability to make comparisons. And so it must be for acts of love or tenderness! Extremes and novelties wake the deepest incursions into the memory strands of the brain. So the test of maturity may be in part to reduce the undue emphases of memories—from births to cruelties and even to death.

Not unrelated: the Coast Guard service is truly lazy because its image is only the bravely spectacular—when a boat or life is saved by crews of men in the service. For the rest of the time, it's a good "idled" job for poets and writers—rather like the fire departments of big cities. Yesterday in our great blow and fog the coast guard might well have circled the harbor constantly. There is no other way of knowing if vessels are dragging their anchors or bearing down on other vessels. The wind being easterly, our own shore was the kindly lee and hence a dozen or more small craft moved from across the harbor to partake of our protection. And we cut many flowers rather than have them tattered in the unprotected garden. Our gulls soon left the water to go inland— one of the best tip-offs of a coming, increased wind. Sometimes the gulls give us wind advice five or six hours before the weathercasters of radio and press.

It is hard for me to sit down during the gale. There is so much to look out for: the length and size of waves, the idiosyncrasies of boats lying at their moorings or anchors, the beach grass bending to the wind—better resistancers than sturdy oaks which fight the wind (I still don't know why we don't use more bamboo as they do in Japan), the pools of rain at bottom of ineptly designed water leaders, and of course the fog in its battle with the sun. I run from one barometer, the recording type, to my thirty-year-old brass one from my first ketch, the Episode, and never stop pondering the coincidence of high tide with the peak of a storm.

Helped Goldies, who leave the island today. I fly down early because delightful, exciting mail and calls from clients have piled up to the point where I get two or three calls each day.

August

Monday and Tuesday, August 1 and 2

A big city interlude. Pleasurable but the adjustment period confusing. While at work—so-called—I thought of Monomoy, the pleasant dinner at victualer Wyler's Chanticleer, the soft-voiced ballad singer at Clem Reynolds' saloon and how in Nantucket no one uses the phrase "I killed time." What an obscene concept that man should murder his precious moments, should be so insufficient to himself that he murders his only possession of real value.

Then I thought, while taking my cold shower, about our prebreakfast dips in the harbor and how I always get an additional close-eye while Maggie is washing, a process that takes a full quarter hour because our bathroom views the garden. I recall Jessamyn West's home north of San Francisco, and particularly her bathtub which has at its side a big picture window looking out at her garden. This is easy elegance, a long bath in a good tub with an inflated pillow and a view of what one loves with intimacy. The only improvement would be two bathtubs so we could bathe, gaze and chat together (Maggie and I, not Jessamyn).

Great conversation at Plaza with publisher Arthur Cohen and his cohorts. We skipped from subject to subject, with paragraphs shortened because our minds flowed.

To Goldies' for breakfast at 7:30 and delighted to be able to report to Maggie that Stef is excited about her day at Hoffman's Camp. An adjustable creature, secure in herself.

Wednesday through Saturday, August 3, 4, 5, 6

These four days on my island are a patch in themselves—starting with sun and warm weather and shifting to easterly and cool breezes with overcast skies, and then today warm and clear with wild canaries in the garden and the flowers, except for roses, at their peak performances. The phlox excite all, and the hydrangeas—unsubtle blooms—gain admiration.

On return I faced my project list: sharpening knives on new soapstone, painting jobs, put on new burgee, cut grass and so forth.

For two days we struggled over a specially designed double-crostic created by neighbor Ann Harmon for Maggie and me. It was the hardest we ever worked on—one of those jobs only solved by allowing intermissions, so that our minds would get fresh gazes at letters and words that had become frozen and rigid.

Alan Norcross, plumber who borrowed my jigsaw and lathe last winter, brought in a beautifully turned, laminated mahogany bowl as thank-symbol for the loan. I showed him the berry bowl set I had made, joining together different woods —maple, mahogany and cherry. It's nearly time for Nick to become friends with the jigsaw and lathe.

Took Ricky Wolff [137] out sailing and after a half hour shoved him off in a mild wind and even sea, on his own. That's the great moment—when responsibility shifts and man meets dangers all on his lonesome.

Read in *Listener* good piece by a well-named gent, Mr. Comfort, telling how in all of Europe children reach maturity sooner now than decades ago. For example, from 1850 to 1950, menarche, the first female menopause, has gotten earlier at rate of one-third to one-half year each decade. Boys tougher to identify, although the moon has not let boys alone, and I have bored many teachers and parents by asking for records of days when boys were "cranky" each month.

Then in some scientific gazette, intrigued to learn that cats do always land on their feet—and the acrobatics are described in detail. Internal gyroscope or balance canal is one we should ape if possible. I guess we have the equipment but it's knocked out of condition by fear, the monkey wrench in many daring, human potentials.

Work on *Privacy and the Law* is more exciting every time I ask laymen: Do you own your own face? What of your parents' faces if they are dead? Does the lawful use of your name or photo for advertising depend on the prestige of the commodity? How would you feel if your pet dog were photographed for the *New York Post* as compared to *Harper's* or *New York Times* or *Fortune?* I think I have learned more law, or at least about the law of privacy, from conversations with laymen than from law books. Incidentally, the best-reasoned opinion I have found was written in Georgia in 1904. Just beautiful, exciting reasoning.

[137] Son of W. Wolff, law partner.

Happy that Estes [138] re-elected by a big vote.

Just asked Maggie whether voices are getting harsher and rougher or does my increasing deafness increase my awareness? All my life I have barred from close intimacy some women and fewer men whose voices jarred me. The voice may well be, with smell, the base of sexual attraction (as color with birds). But now I think I am more disturbed than formerly by rasping, grating sounds uttered by children and adults! I prefer less wisdom in a good tone and pitch.

Sunday, August 7

Sail, swims, worked in shed; we painted canvas on porch. Beautiful day for lunch in garden on movable table cart, which we had to move to get tree shade; tucked up rose branches, a chore I detest; took Nick to shop and gave him his first lesson on the lathe—first on pine, fresh and naughty, showing its objections by roughness and splinters and even turning against sand paper as if it were an enemy.

Made up my mind to start using my numerous cards and notes to write the opening passages of *Privacy and the Law.* I'm excited about it—maybe too excited to do an easy reading book for laymen.

Tuesday and Wednesday, August 9 and 10

A two-day jaunt from Monomoy, after a morning cutting grass and working on a friendly piece of walnut—teaching Nicholas the magic of inventing contours on a lathe with the design taking control of the chisels. Drove past the meadows and quiet changing marshes, and plane to the office. The

[138] Senator Kefauver.

European travelers all back, some in love with England, some with French food, and some of the sad group not in love at all. Good mail in and out. To dinner with Alan and Paula. Entranced by my friend Compton Mackenzie complimenting me by saying I had some of his love of life.

The next morning enjoyed two breakfasts—the first at 7:15 at the Goldies', where all is as it should be, serene and contented. What have they to trouble them except that Joan and Irving have never heard sound, not even the chirp of a bird or the bark of a dog. But Steffie gay and adjustable as children of the deaf must be in the first experiences with cooperation—the family. Then to Vanderbilt with Arthur Cohen, the publisher, whose mind is as random and floating as was that of Jerome Frank. To office and to lunch with another client and many new ventures: magazines to bras to divorce.

Read report of Ike's press conference. Thought about what teachers of syntax and grammar say when reading such confusions of words.

In *Yachts & Yachting* learned that the compass rose was once called Flower of the Wind. Magnificent issue of *New Scientist* celebrating 300th anniversary of Royal Society of London—started before the Great Plague and just after the Civil War. The Society represents the best in tradition and ideas.

Why was I such a scientific ignoramus all my life? The literature was available, and our land was not isolated from the source of theoretical knowledge—England, or of development techniques—Germany. With travel so slow, the Renaissance took decades to amble from Florence to London. But even in my youth we had ten-day boats to Liverpool and the cable. I have lost a precious hunk of thrills. I only hope the grandchildren don't duplicate my errors and waste. So I bring to Monomoy to replace Davey Crockett and the Sarnoff-Paley Gun fetish for children, a set of lenses and the sun-powered

cigarette lighter which Marie gave me a year or so ago. I miss
Marie.

Friday, August 12 and Saturday, August 13

Back on the job experimenting with plexiglas for roofing;
sandpapers for a piece of wood on the lathe; battling rust—
man's enemy—which costs our nation more than we spend
for education. I think it's close to $10 billion a year. I read
somewhere that it costs $80 million annually to replace rusted
mufflers. Now they may lick it, for the sly devil oxygen has
been named as the penetrater of iron and introducer of rust.

New rose is a beauty. M. suggests we replace our thirty-
year-old roses since improvements in size, color and anti-
mildew are so great. I wish man had improved as much.

Monday, August 15

Befogged, so good for writing and reading. High spot: to
watch drawing of lucky number at First National for Buggy
Oldsmobile—which Jim Lamb, our carpenter, won. It's good
that a townsman won the car.

Took a hundred or so books to Atheneum; [139] borrowed a
grommet machine at shipyard to make windbreak for Maggie's favorite flower bed in case of a big blow; bought a new
hybrid cross between plane and rasp; put up gull wire on
bronze fittings given to me by new neighbor—cleric Thomas;
visited with Thomases in their new home, Maggie bringing
them a bouquet; allowed Nick to row alone and watched.
Otherwise the usual swims, and gazing out on harbor and
garden. Made new mahogany cleat for hold-down for swim-

[139] Public library.

ming ladder. Ate enough of Arlene's [140] good muffins and cookies to satisfy hunger without waistline expansion.

Very quiet on all fronts, with all couples off island—and only Nick and Kath as family neigbhors. Called up by office a few times, but nothing to take me down this week—and next week I'm not allowed to go what with the biochemists from Woods Hole coming over, and a party for Maggie's pleasure on my birthday.

Sent Ferber a telegram out west somewhere.

Wednesday, August 17

Spoke to Murphy, the Radio-TV man on the island. Almost every house is defiled by one of his TV antennae. It's nearly as unseemly as Burford, England, that village kept intact since the fifteenth century but now besmudged with antennae standing out of the thatched roofs. Here a few folk order their antennae before they have a receiving set. The prestige symbol is the rod on the roof. Soon they will be built into the sets—but this may take a decade or so. In the meanwhile I suggested that he coordinate the antennae with the captain's walks that rest across the ridge poles of many of our old saltbox homes. I see no reason why a vogue cannot be created for removal of the hideous metal frames reaching a dozen feet above the roof and submerging them in a neat captain's walk.

Good brisk weather, so back to our life on the water. As I write early in the day, I wait restlessly for news from Connie who once more is in the clutches of the medicos.

Then Rose tells us Connie phoned and all good news. Nothing else matters today.

[140] Arlene Cliette, artist-cook.

Thursday, August 18

Dig holes for fertilizer and transplanting three poplars. Propelled in part by memory of 1929 when our domain was all beach grass and we planted dozens of pines sent by the Commonwealth of Massachusetts—about six inches high each. Now we have a dell, enclosed in a forest.

I listen to the press conference at the White House and our wordless President. Too bad that plus his simple simplicities he does not have an ear for words and phrases and cadences. With the advent of TV and radio, leaders of the future will need the zeal and instinct for the right word in the right place. Lincoln had it and only had to use it on rare public occasions. And I don't mean humor or Castro-like effusions of the tongue.

The cello concert last night in graceful Unitarian Church was without great feeling on the part of music writers other than Chopin. But I recalled my cello days and how, during one of my mother's desperate anti-T.B. hibernations, my sentimental aunt, with whom I lived, dreamt up the idea that I surprise my mother on her return by playing the cello. Why not trombone or fencing, I'll never know. So sure enough, to wet eyes, I played the "Traumerei" as mama came down the stairs in my grandparents' home on East 120th Street—one of the many homes of my youth.

My real musical education was "supering" at the Met while at high school—fifty cents a night, but I learned my Wagner and much of all the operas. My great roles were a priest in *Tosca*, a soldier in *Lohengrin* and a waiter with fake champagne in *Die Fledermaus*. So I had it, and this may explain why opera now provides me with little more than the pride of recognition of motifs and the flattering joy of the precognition of notes to come—all of little relation to the emotional values of notes kissing the ears.

Friday, August 19

Another sunless day, and people living in single rooms can't take it and thus leave the island. A tough season for the Nantucketers—boat strike for first half of summer, inordinate fog since August began.

Mag [141] came over from Woods Hole. Connie and Mike's plane stranded them at Hyannis.

Found a pleasant secretary—Mrs. Leske—and she took a batch of copy work on new *Privacy* book. Brad [142] came out and I raised again the desperate need on the island for new, young leadership. If there were only one lawyer—dedicated (which is different from having affection) and possessing a touch of zeal—to let the island face its truly overwhelming problems.

To cocktail party at Perry's [143] for Oscar Silverman [144]— nothing but scholars and professors. Felt as if I had crashed.

To bed early. Awoke at 4 A.M., went downstairs, grabbed first unread book—Bos Crowther's life of Louis B. Mayer. Entertained in part because I have met most of the tawdry who ran the movies from 1909 on. Surely L. B. M. was a meager and indecent human who should not be forgiven because he was the Rajah of Hollywood. I fear Bos has been so close to movies for so many years on the *Times* that he has been coated with the celluloid smear and his feelings have been desensitized. He's too forgiving, just as Crosby,[145] with

141 Sister, Magdalen Stetten.
142 Bradford Johnson, Episcopal minister.
143 Professor Ten Eyck Perry.
144 Professor at University of Buffalo.
145 John Crosby, *Herald Tribune* columnist.

his remaining indignation at TV, is reluctant to put the onus where it belongs—on Paley and Sarnoff. If leaders are to get credit for their good deeds, why should there not be protests at the evils they do? Crosby, Lippmann and the editorial writer of the *Herald Tribune* could alone create a revolution in TV by addressing themselves to Paley and Sarnoff—and I'd add Goldenson, who is a leader in the gutter of sadism, which Paley and Sarnoff use as a justification for their defaults.

Friday, August 19 and Saturday, August 20

"Cleo," the new hurricane, needed watching. Took out atlas and charted course. At 6 P.M., 300 miles off Richmond, Virginia—too far out to tend by shore radio, so rely on airplanes—moving 20 miles an hour northward. It seems to be on about 70° longitude so we may get it. By 6 P.M. told it will come at sunrise. So to bed, intent on early rise so as not to miss the excitement. Up early—clear sky and obviously "Cleo" went to sea, or blew herself out, or was evaporated by the upper cold air jet stream.

These kids are interesting and would be so wonderful if it weren't for adults. Steffie heard from a seven-year-old friend that if she does something wrong she'll be punished by God. Her friend gets this utter corruption from her parents—and so it goes down the line to Nick and Kathie. Horrors—so remote from the truth that man pays somehow for his own errors and his own errors are for the most part peculiarly cut to his own custom orders—and only a few that spell reward or punishment by society's standards. Private morality is much higher and more sensitive than societal virtue. But even our kids are in the grip of values created not by themselves out of their own group relationships, but by others.

Sunday, August 21

Nick at stage where he must, just must, see the inside of everything—wonderful fun to be with in this mood. Also starting to ask questions about mysteries of life, and I don't mean just birth and death. There is nothing greater or more interesting than all that lies between. So we puzzle about sounds of wire vibrations on the pier, magnets, magnification, and parts of motors.

A truly elegant party. The Hardy brothers[146] and Doc Ryder[147] threw it at the beautiful Hardy barn. Orchestra, about 100 people, all dolled up, and a good mixture of natives and the Larsen[148]-Sconset coterie. The Larsenites only *seem* more secure with their overlay of *savoir-faire,* but their innards are apparent. They are neither fighters nor martyrs. I prefer the fighters to the martyrs, for the martyrs are fighters who want to lose or at least enjoy defeat.

Big parties are very risky—it's so easy to be stuck with a bore.

Monday, August 22

My birthday tomorrow. Another year has gone with goods and bads but the balance as always on the plus side. I guess life is only a game of having more pluses than minuses.

Only too late have I developed a clearing house of the mind. Only too long have I delayed making my choice of what may be my last cruising sailboat. Only too inept have I been in finding and latching on to kindred minds like Russell Leffingwell and Marie Jahoda and the late Heywood

146 John and Robert Hardy, Island businessmen.
147 Harold Ryder of Ryder's Market, champion golfer.
148 Roy Larsen of *Time* and *Life.*

Broun and Jerome Frank. But my luck continues to ride me and vice versa. A few teeth have said goodbye—what with my jaw weakened rather than strengthened by verbalism. My ears slowly but surely resent sounds and especially the waves that are generated by the chat of human beings.

But roots get deeper and firmer in Nantucket and at the corner of Washington Square and Fifth Avenue.

The kids all have their troubles and ride them with grace, and Maggie continues to act as professional shopper for the Delhi contingent—looking for a shipable broom for a culture that has not yet reached the Handle Age, or razor blades or collapsible swimming pool for David and Debbie—all of whom we plan to visit next February, between the monsoons and the furnace sun heat. Maggie's revised *In A Word* comes out next month, and tomorrow I must be gracious about a goddamn awful birthday party for forty people on the beach—a party for the benefit of all present except me, a detester of the anniversary concept and more particularly anniversary presents and parties. Anniversaries of birth or death are little more than excuses for special observances, rather than considerations hour by hour.

So I'm seventy-two—an exciting age for one who still runs to the pier and goes up steps two at a time (no longer three) and has open pores which enjoy a rich, wet sweat.

Tuesday, August 23

Beach picnic. Six Stettens in for overnight, Gumports with their tribe of five, neighbors to left and right—a total of 80 hamburgers, 40 franks, 30 ears of corn, all of which Arlene and Rose,[150] our treasures, handled without the faintest moaning.

[149] Rose Saunders, Bessies' maid and friend.

Card, telegrams and presents galore—and embarrassing. Wines, cognacs, ties, games, books, candies, goodies—plus the tooth of a whale to carve and handsome bindings for clippings on *Touch Wood* in case it is reviewed. Nick buys me, on his own, a set of tools for the boat; and Dea and Jo [150] send me a letter addressed as usual, "Dear Junior."

Weather perfect, with a dozen or more kids on pier, floats, in water and boats—like the best of a Tivoli. I have put Rose's primitive painted clam shell on my desk for an ash tray.

Finally cut broom for Jean—with a dog-tooth splice, and bolts and nuts, so as to ship by mail in length permitted by postage rules.

To bed weary, and happy day is over so I can get back to normal life of sweat and splinters tomorrow.

Wednesday, August 24

Finished Harry S. Truman's book and enjoyed its pert, frank observations on indecisiveness of Stevenson and others. Amused that we have so much in common: no liking for hard "licker," prefer white to red wine, fast-walking (120 paces to the minute), early-rising, food preferences though eat nearly everything, special interest in United States history and biographies.

Heard Walter Lippmann on radio interview with Howard K. Smith. Worthwhile—though I do not agree with his reasons for voting for Dewey and Eisenhower, and do understand why he was off F. D. R. Naturally, after having a key to the White House from Woodrow Wilson days on, he never understood why he and Eugene Meyer, men of ability and integrity, were not deemed of value to the F. D. R. programs.

[150] The Houlihans, former maid and nurse.

Weather perfect—barometer up. Temperature of air and water at 8 A.M. identic. A rare but wonderful sensation.

Hours at desultory occupation—polishing a whale's tooth. Will try to etch it with some acid instead of engraving with three-cornered sailor's needle.

Party at Craig's [151]—warm and friendly with neighbors of our shore.

Tooth pulled, and stepped on a bee while clipping hedge— neither carrying memory of pain for any real amount of time.

Privacy book in very, very rough draft, all typed here and in New York—about 80 per cent complete. Now the part I hate: redoing, reorganization, re-arrangement. The prefix "re" is not my favorite if it applies to anything I have done by my lonely self.

Thursday, August 25

Generous letter from Tom Lamont, and he is considerate enough to let me know that Russell has asked, as soon as he is feeling up to it, to have someone read *Touch Wood* to him and that he is amused by it. This makes the volume worth-while to me—preferable to the opinion of any newspaper book critic—although I hope the *Times* looks on it with favor, for without the *Times*, in our congested best-seller-list culture, few books get wide popular acceptance.

Made extensive inquiries since I thought of etching my whale's tooth with acid instead of drawing scrimshaw on it as is the usual practice. Bill Coffin, Dr. Vallett my dentist, and others report briefly: "It's never been done." As if that were a human answer to anything.

[151] Mrs. William Craig of Baltimore.

Friday, August 26 and Saturday, August 27

Maggie's pleasure in reading *To Kill a Mockingbird* made me pick it up instead of articles on world peace, tariff. Read half and enjoyed it, not only as a picture of Alabama but because of intimate, subtle portrayal of the difficulty of a lawyer who acts as a lawyer. How few really believe every person is entitled to a lawyer.

Must write Alan about the Scotland Yard purchase of a copy of *Lady Chatterly*. Now we will have a test of the new British statute and although Penguin will win—by judge or jury—it still won't mean that "corruption" of readers is related to literary flavor or style. When do lawyers allow science to be used by the law?

Sunday, August 28

This summer's treasure gal—Arlene—cook, painter, bottle-washer extraordinary, after being kidded, wrote out a menu when I asked if it was worthwhile leaving my good book for mere food.

Monomoy's Touch Wood Dining Room

Dessert Menu—Choice of:

Watermelon slices
Blueberries
Ice cream:
chocolate
watermelon
lime
Butterscotch cookies

Breakfast:
Juice or Berries
Eggs any style
Muffins
Biscuits or fried dough
Cereal—Hot or Cold
Coffee   Milk   Tea

Mass. Food tax included.

Big to-do in Sconset Casino. A Negro girl wanted to enter her dog in a pet contest, was accepted and then given her twenty-five-cent fee back and rejected. Her mother wrote a tender and affectionate letter to the *Inquirer* and *Mirror*. Then I found myself in the midst of it all—a proposed picket line and a real problem.

Monday, August 29

Friendly housewarming party at neighbor Thomas's—met the quiet elegant of Sconset. Delighted when picket line withdrawn from Casino because of stupid refusal to a Negro girl of eight or nine to enter her dog in the pet show. How slow it is to nudge bigoted folkways—but with Nat Benchley [152] and Wendell Howes,[153] we use rational attitudes to reduce heat of prejudices.

Trip down long but pleasant.

Monday, 7:30, for breakfast at Joan's. They are in high fettle and Irv is deluged with work.

Found no interest in election; saw *Inherit the Wind* preview with H. F. P.[154]—good portrayal of Darrow by Spencer

[152] Author.
[153] Police Chief.
[154] Harriet F. Pilpel, partner.

Tracy, although Clarence was never harsh, for his glands led him to forgive all people and look for their love. Interesting that he lost this case, as he did so many, in the courts, but won in public education and esteem.

Wednesday, August 31

Much excitement. Received copies of *In A Word,* Maggie's new book, on which Leonard Harris [155] has done a great job; last night dinner at "21" with TV producer of psychiatric shows, then to Mahoney's [156] where refreshed old friendship with Marc Connelly; [156a] today much client work and fun. Letters on *Touch Wood* are kind; review in *Library Journal* pleased publishers greatly; Calderone of Schooner Tradition and of skating boats drops in from Caribbean; lunch with Andrew and Johnston (young lawyer now head of Railway Express); ran into ex-Adlai managers—now for Kennedy. Plane to New Bedford, taxi to Hyannis; organized party of eight to get fishing boat to Nantucket where we arrived at 2:30 A.M. Mrs. Arthur Dean on junket—adding much to gaiety. Maggie asleep—but hops up cheerful—gets food for me, talk, talk, talk and then to sleep thinking of R. L. who is returning from hospital, so his housekeeper told me.

[155] Publisher, Channel Press.
[156] Margaret Mahoney, Carnegie Foundation.
[156a] Playwright.

September

Friday, September 2

Visited Sarah and Sidney—left wet-eyed. They have sold the house which they have owned here for more than eighty years. We offered to buy it so that during their lives they could have the needed chauffeur, handy man to do chores. But it ain't money, just responsibility—what with Sarah finding it most difficult to climb steps and Sidney unable to see enough to drive a nail. He, as I do, receives most of his "home-reward" from doing chores—painting, putting in a new window pane and all those delights which are converted into devils of compulsion in a rented home. M. and I talk on way home—if either of us dies the other will sell the Nantucket house, and treat it as a great and longish Episode of many decades. Sarah has read *Touch Wood* to Sidney and they say they enjoyed it, thinking Penelope was someone in my office. I wish I could see more of P.—or, more honestly, let her enter more of this diary.

The lie detector, says *Science News*, may aid in predicting likely candidates for a coronary. Well, glad to hear one worthy use of this damnably attractive invention—dangerous beyond measure for the courts and justice. At this moment the worst of its effects is the increasing idea that refusal to use it is proof of guilt.

Labor Day Week End
September 3, 4, 5, 1960

Zip in the air. Good days for anything from chores to talk. Work on antigull program and may try red paint which is supposed to be a deterrent for some birds. Several hours with neighbor Caplans [157]—I do think this island is getting him; she's been bitten from the start. They are perfect neighbors— friendly and interesting but great respecters of man's major right, the right to be left alone.

Read page proof of Birth Control brief for Supreme Court. H. F. P. worked like a slave on it. This ends, I believe and hope, my forty-five-year legal battle on the court front, for breakdown of Comstock laws. The argument will not take place until February since Fowler Harper—counsel-in-chief— is off to Africa and will ask for delay.

These are the days when we do nothing and have no time to do it.

[157] Mr. and Mrs. Lewis Caplan, New Haven lawyer and his wife.

Thursday, September 8

New York City not too bad with fine weather—though I slept badly as I always do when alone. To the Goldies' for breakfast and then a full day at the office, which is just about at the end of the summer routines. Several business bust-ups —really no different than a marriage divorce. The basic point of law is, as always, establish good will if possible to reduce the scars. Brief in U.S. Supreme Court in Chicago police brutality case (*Monroe* vs. *Pape*) finally in print, and the Chicago lawyers did a fine job. I feel guilty that I did not do more of the work.

To dinner with Schwartzes junior and senior. Saw Rhoda [158] —that embryonic novelist; sent Sir Harold Hartley [159] a letter about Ray Harwood [160] who is off for England; watched "retired" Herb work at his pleasant desk. Cleaned up a mass of mail; called and found R. L. comfortable.

Friday, Saturday, and Sunday, September 9, 10 and 11

This week end much happened that I neither foresaw nor designed. To Manchester, Vermont for Second Circuit Judicial Conference—all federal judges and some lawyers. Was enriched by visit with Connecticut and Vermont barristers, whose law service is still a profession and a mission. They have not been degraded by keeping time sheets—the billing art of the plumber. They know that a profession deals in

[158] Rhoda St. James, typist, writer.
[159] Head of British Electrical Board.
[160] Of Harper's.

time, but more rare and important, wisdom—which arises un-regulated by clock, and is often born in split seconds. I have never kept a time sheet in my life unless by order of a court in a receivership or the like. Met young New York City lawyers who not only resent the Time Sheet Life but know it is an instrument of cheating one client for the benefit of another.

The program on evidence was rich with pedagogues who could articulate. More vision and daring than in previous years—maybe due to shift of committee chairmen. This year advance papers were sent out inviting a thoughtful audience. But the arguments centered on uniformity which I'm opposed to in nearly all of life or law, for I know very little that is so definitely and completely explored as to permit a nationwide pattern. So I asked, "Do you want a Uniform Divorce Law?" "Sure," was the answer. Then I dirtied the query with—"How? Only for adultery as in New York? or no divorce as South Carolina? or mental cruelty as in Mexico?" Then each one pulled back and agreed that whenever experimentation has not yet ended, he prefers the waste, irritation and duplication involved in using the fifty states as experimental laboratories.

Good weather. Regretted I could not hitch to New York. Plane to La Guardia, helicopter to Idlewild, then plane to Nantucket. Had not planned on helicopter—and a little ashamed I had not been in one before. But I have so many other firsts ahead of me that my chagrin fast evaporated. The descent was like the swing of a Ferris wheel carriage. I liked it, and the service was exceptional—in part because there was no hostess on board. I wish airlines would think of planes as transportation and not as imitation of Night Clubs.

Vermont was a separate nation and its people still show it by curt, brief wit and by a quiet friendly mood. Reminded by British barrister of the man who took his dog to have the tail clipped off so that when mother-in-law arrived there would not even be a wag of welcome.

Our shore is busy—the Bessies closed their house, Roger's tenant, Peter Feibleman,[161] left and so did Joan's tenants. So we old folk are here alone and love it, and busy on chores for the kid's houses and preparing to close our own. Weather warm—no fires—but all on good nerves watching course of Donna. We do not want to miss a hurricane and will stay till Saturday if it will come here.

Monday, September 12

Miss, not Mrs. Donna came in for a brief visit—brief as visits from her family go. Advance announcements of her coming were ample, so we got out her own special red rug. Brought in the sailboat, hauled up the dinghy, put storm shutters on big windows in all houses but ours—for I'd rather see her in transit even though she, hating plate glass, might have been offended at my insolence and lack of fear of her power.

The storm came and went all in a day; we enjoyed battening down and the excitement of preparation. We even defied the lady by taking a swim off the end of the pier at the top of the blow—which went beyond our old anemometer which registered only to 60 mph.

Every guess from every station as to wind direction was totally in error at all times for Nantucket. Most stations gave incorrect reports steadily—many a station reading a report at noon which may have been true at 8 A.M.—and this did a great disservice. I rather think that the Weather Bureau should take over all stations—networks at least—every hour on the hour when there's a disaster ahead, or a threat of one.

[161] Novelist.

We both used nerves seldom in use—so it was odd fun. Damage we will check tomorrow. Roof of shed I can see, is off.

Tuesday, September 13

This is the day after the tenseness of a hurricane. Our island showed winds up to 70 mph, and high tides—but we are the opposite of an estuary and so there is no bottling up of waters. One boat was driven up on bulkhead next to Coast Guard Station, and a picture of that scene would be less than kind to the C.G.

The day was calm, not in comparison to yesterday, but serene by any standards. So we unbundled, removed the flower protections, window protections on Roger's house and the many precautions that showed up over the entire estate.

A pleasant day—better than coming back to light after going through a long tunnel such as Simplon; different from that half hour in bed when we come back from our unconscious journeys once more, to meet up with the life of our five senses; something like the semiconscious, physically-spent, semilethargic peace after love making. It was a little like each of these and we had the additional relief and pride at having nature's effort to lick us fail—though it left us with humility and reluctance to boast of victory.

In the evening Leila [162] and Bert [163] were here for celebration banquet—from steak to souffle à la Arlene—and then we went to Mooneys' [164] to talk over the Primary vote—meeting Republican Selectman Sidney Killen and a friend from West

[162] Leila McKnight of Washington.
[163] Bert Bell of Washington.
[164] Robert Mooney, Island Representative to Massachusetts Assembly and photographer wife, Lee.

Virginia. The Washington girls are violent-speaking, heated, professional party Democrats, and I wondered whether I'm exchanging heat for caution in my eighth decade.

Worked hard with joy of labor-sweat, followed by dips in cool harbor water. Took up duffel, anchors and boats; Maggie painting as she will each day this week. Old Man Paint is a great burden in economies needing beauty; it is disagreeable only when cleaning brushes, and satisfying because results are visible and complete.

Thursday, September 15

Closing up a house or season or an episode need be neither sad nor happy. The emotion may well depend on what we are going to do next. To go to daily law-advising, to our Washington Square trees, to our city pictures and furniture is no bad break. Much of the impact of the change, I do believe, depends on weather and chores to be undertaken more than anything else. One more day and my thirty-fifth summer on this blessed island will end—thirty-one years in this house with a view of the town, the churches and the lighthouse.

At Green Coffee Pot for lobster in wine. The waitress says to Margaret, "Just a minute, Honey," and we agree that "Honey" is small town usage—never heard at "21" or the Plaza.

Friday, September 16

Last chores finished—shop cleaned, tools oiled, outside thermometer put inside, floor boards of metal dinghy repaired—swims, and all at peace.

To Chatfield Taylors' [165] for small party—not all Democrats. These folk already disturbed by Communist base in Cuba— all worried what the White House can now do after a year and a half of naive behavior which virtually invited the Communists into this hemisphere.

Looked for new sport coat at shop but afraid to select one. All my life I've despised shopping and in fact am proud of only a few items I have bought—my wood-carved Borgatta "Jonah and the Fish," my table saw, my Hong Kong lifetime shoes, a black brief case and maybe a dozen other selections. Oh yes—my hand drill and sander.

I think again of the autobiography of Lovatt Dickson, the head of Macmillan, and truly believe my youth was essentially like his—though never hungry for food, I was usually desolate for a friend. I recall no confidants in my youth. Not that I was a sensitive lad as was the author of that great book *The Ante-Room*—but I was frightened and lonely for sure. Told Maggie that in 1910, when I decided to study law at night, there was not a single member of the Bar, known to me and of status, whom I dared go to for a chat or advice. I'm not sorry for myself—only regretful.

Saturday, September 17

Nantucket peaceful, and we drove through the village once more.

Violent shift. Plane to New York City. At Vineyard agent of airline came on board in a scolding mood. Eight pieces of baggage had to be removed—as if it were the passengers' fault. We volunteered our one bag, and a lady with $12.00 of overweight was last to let her bag follow. So off to New York in clear skies.

[165] Distinguished public servant and wife, old Nantucketers.

In city, apartment and Square look at ease—but Maggie has difficulty making shifts of settings except when traveling abroad. To office and worked all afternoon going through several messes of mail. To Goldies for dinner and all in good spirits. Maggie went home—tired out and to bed; I to Bessies and chatted till near midnight.

One interesting bit. A taxi driver hopes Wagner and Ike drop dead—the kind of wish no one would have in Nantucket, a bit too violent. But he's sore for wrong reason—tax on fares. Quietly explained how he and companies could make a fortune if English cabs were allowed on streets—35 miles on a gallon, spin on a dime, go fast enough. Saving in gas alone (difference of one-third of gas bills) would give great relief. Moreover there should be sharing of cabs as in other big cities. This chatty but thinking driver turned around and said, "You're right."

New restaurant on 8th Street. Tried it out. Viennese food— run by two entertainers—good.

Monday, September 19

Rain, but weather means little in New York City. The city is as confused as I ever recall seeing it. No sober leadership on problem of visiting dictators. Should we let them roam our nation? If so, at their peril? Should New York City spend the $3 million a week needed for protection (why not let them roam)? What of press and TV that are not reporting but making the stories? Who can talk to us—now that Ed Murrow has been boxed and the presidential candidates don't want to take a chance on guiding our people?

Tuesday, September 20

Surprise! Penelope returns from overseas and walks in without a notice or warning. She looks healthy but a mile tall —as tall people who lose weight always do. And this got us into a discussion of the variety of height and weight of people in different climates and areas of the earth. P. tells me of a recent study in our Department of Agriculture which related height of men and women to college education. Absurd, she says, even though statistics indicate two inches increase over sixty years ago; and that present college undergraduates are about an inch taller than their parents; and sons weigh five to ten pounds and daughters two to five pounds more than parents. What absurd course the mind of man will travel! College is irrelevant, I'm sure. What of the eight-foot-high tribe in Africa—without even a primary school? But they may mean that families which send offspring to college have different food, calories and environment.

P. tells me of drugs that reduce fear in cats and rats— or mice, she wasn't too sure. Easy to test animals, she says, by electric shock training, after creating prestige for food or some object. Not so easy with man—a more sensitive, thank God, guinea pig.

Just heard Russell is home and doing handsomely, and that Dave Loth is in hospital with tendon operation. I devised a new legal theory to sue Roger Angell, his tennis opponent, who placed the ball where Dave had to hurt himself to reach it. Theory no good, says Dave, because on the return Dave made his point.

Thursday, September 22

One of those phoney religious office-closings—not for spiritual purposes but, in fact, in derogation of true religion. As one who has never worshipped or belonged to a religious body I should think that sectarian religious people would do away with general closings for religious holidays—allowing those who need a day for worship to have it for worship. Our present mores laugh at true religion of the spirit.

To office—saw clients, went through mail; then to Plaza, on way giving Ed Murrow a hitch—he's low in spirit; ran into Drew Pearson, high in spirit, and hope to see him again tomorrow; lunch with Ann Ronell—who has finished her revised "Martha" for Met; then using Plaza for office, doped out plans for our Book on Year 2000 with Roseman and Tella.

But the big item is the story in *The New Yorker* of fraud of Benton, Adler and Hutchins in the marketing of the so-called "Great Books." They change the words of Milton, Shakespeare and Carlyle in their marketing. How come these Madison Avenue Boys did not rewrite the Bible? Will our press dare pick up this shocking incident of alleged scholars, selling top scholarship by doctoring up the writings of the great? They doctored: "A good book is the precious life blood of a master spirit" by Milton to a "Great Book" in order to make money on the sale of socalled "Great Books" series.

Friday, September 23

Comfortable day. Discussed with Penelope the reason why Jews have more eye strain and myopia than other people. Explained to P. that Jews, despite Hitler, are not a race; but she says they may be affected by deep reading habits of ancestors. This, I return, is a flattering idea—but she, a fairish Unitarian, will check for the truth.

Then with Jock Lawrence [166] at his table at "21" with his braintruster Frank Taylor.[167] There we flirted with new big business techniques to get cross-fertilization of department heads, who should have time to do "nothing" but think; and the stupidity of most of the reports to stockholders.

Back to office—gazing at East River without a tug boat or barge for a long stretch of time.

Home for dinner and peace at 2 Fifth Avenue.

Monday, September 26

Out to dinner with Maggie at Sea Fare. Ran into Dave Dubinsky [168] and his bride. Haven't chatted with him for years, and although he had to run off early, he's still an invigorator for me. Then home for show—Nixon-Kennedy. Quite mediocre. Neither smiled; neither showed a sense of history or a big dream for the future. I guess they were both nervous because it had been played up as a big show. It wasn't much—as usual too many subjects, too little time, too many questions. I wish the questioners were not conditioned, as are TV and news men, to posing the dirty question—as at presidential press conferences.

Penelope sends me *Science News* clipping on blood pressure of butlers, and the amazing statement that high blood pressure is a concomitant of persons in personal service. Bad thinking—it's got nothing to do with the service. I suggest

[166] Public relations expert.
[167] Public relations expert.
[168] Head of I.L.G.W.U.

it's that personal service attracts that type or that it's true of all subservient types.

Read some about carbon 14 and testing for age of man's artifacts. I like this radium waste test, but admire more the man who computed archaeological dates by measuring over-laid deposits of salt. And why not? Age can be told by rings of trees or the deposits of retreating ice sheets. Now I'm told the first peasant farmer lived about 3000 B.C. And how did people exist before then—as nomads or only hunters?

Tuesday, September 27

Bundles of good events—review of *Touch Wood* in *Boston Herald* begs for next year's volume; Dallas invites me November 12 for Book and Author Luncheon; Los Angeles wants to know if I can go there; Alan reads and reports with helpful suggestions on editing of *Privacy;* Brett [169] and Hart [170] invite me to Macmillan's for lunch; Alice Hughes [171] wants to do a piece on Maggie and me; papers come in on Northampton professor case and raise exciting point of law.

Point of law is simple and never fully tested. Warrant for search is on printed form, and cop merely swore he had reason to believe a crime had been committed—with no statement of basis for such belief. If this is good law, no home is safe.

So Russia and Castro are intent on harassing the UN, and we are in trouble; for even in a free-for-all to capture the minds of the uncommitted, we have no plan for persuasion and rely too much on money. We lack evangelical zeal.

Wrote Jack Kennedy he might, on problem of conflict be-

[169] George Brett, then President, Macmillan Publishing Co.
[170] Al Hart, top editor: Macmillan Publishing Co.
[171] Columnist, King Features.

tween government and private business, refer to fire departments which originally were run for profit. I once had a poster which read, "No Money, No Squirty." Later we realized the city could do the job of fire department service better than could the profit motive. Also suggested he should list all the instances of government in business that came through Republicans. Hoover put over the RFC, a vast government bank, and Dawes, the Republican vice-president, got a loan for his bank of more than $80 million; the Belmont group built the Cape Cod Canal and when it flopped, got Uncle Sam to buy it for about $20 million—and so goes the list. I want to keep the government out of business except where the differential in service or cost is so great as to make private enterprise too costly. Kennedy should explore the list and cost of Republican hypocrisy on this level.

Wednesday, September 28

Two good items and one to offset. Hurricane Donna brought to Nantucket, I read, many unusual birds—an immature, white-tailed tropical bird from Bermuda, also a sooty tern, whatever that is. They don't say if the easiest blown (or most adventurous) are male or female. After all it was Eve who was daring enough to grab for the apple. But thus does animal life proliferate on our continent without the use of boats or planes.

For dinner we went to E. F. Like old times. She was not harassed at all except by the Kennedy-Nixon show which lacked spirit and even a human approach. Begged her to write one of her great letters to the press.

But then to see movie—Red Lewis' *Elmer Gantry*. A horror. Maybe the subtle story of revivalism in churches can't be told for millions of dollars. A $300,000 production would have been compelled to be subtle and sensitive.

Molly's [172] pie offset the movie.

Thursday, September 29

Final talk with Phillips of Columbia, the creator of the Frankfurter book. He wants to do me. Why should I—vanity, publicity? Surely I can carry on my negligible campaigns in books and over the air. But being vain, I may be easily seduced.

To lunch at Morgan Guaranty with Henry [172a] and Tom.[173] As I told them—this is the nearest I'll get to an honorary degree. What an education I got on world and domestic affairs. They seemed intrigued by my new approach to mineral wealth of underdeveloped lands, and say they will follow up. Also cleared things away with Tom to go to Cass about publishing young Tommy's letters, with a background chapter on the family traditions and standards on which the young lad built his wise observations.

Saw Connie at hospital. She's coming along fine. She has bounce and made us happy.

To Plaza for dinner with Dreyfusses [174] and had the pleasure of finding Judge Friendly there. How lucky we are to have him on the Appellate Bench. A rare person—big business inclinations, but he will be educated to Jerome Frank's, not Learned Hand's, approach to civil liberty.

172 Molly, cook for Edna Ferber.
172a Henry Alexander.
173 Thomas Lamont.
174 Henry and Doris, California industrial designers.

Friday, September 30

Law, law, law all day. All secrets that are exciting but none belong to me—even to enter in a vault for future reference.

Lunch with Pat Beresford [175] and Alice Hughes and Maggie. Maggie was interviewed by Alice for a syndicated feature article, and I was delighted to discover another facet of Alice, her knowledge of the manufacture of words—not by Madison Avenue or Winchell (their words won't fit into any culture for any length of time), but changes, errors and shifts of meaning such as Maggie writes about in *In A Word*. We still dare people to look up "fastidious" or invite them to get to the source of "serendipity."

Helped out Ginsburg on his life of Sumner and the Vice Society with a few stories of my battles with that antisocial frustrated group.

Then to meet representatives of Libraries—and if I were not a basic optimist, I'd be in despair at lack of imagination and courage of those who manage the books of our nation. An informed girl from the library field was truly shocked when I asked her why they did not get a librarian invited to a White House dinner with our president? Why only banking, big business, military and government types?

Lovely inscription from Teddy—my favorite direct, extrovert gal lawyer—in the book she did with H. F. P., *Rights and Writers*.

Still upset about Connie. Tough going.

[175] Patricia Beresford, public relations.

October

Saturday, October 1

Reviews of *Touch Wood* most pleasing—*Christian Science Monitor*'s Paul Freund truly generous. I can't say I'm not disturbed that my friends at the *Times* tell me that my acceptance of Galindez inquiry and my opposition to Matthews on Castro have put me on list of unmentionables. This is the first of my dozen books not reviewed in the daily and Sunday *Times*.

So I'll survive even though the *Times* is not only our greatest paper but is the only method of reaching in print book readers in masses.

In evening to Florie and Andrew Loebl with the Gumports. Steve G. has a restless mind of the type I enjoy. Walked downtown for a mile in crisp wind. In the morning I approached a basket with a piece of silver paper I had carried a block or so in my antilitter campaign. I threw it in the basket but a gust of wind picked it out. For several hundred yards the paper dogged my footsteps. I crossed the street; it kept pace. And when I turned the corner it turned with me. Why? A challenge to see if I'd pick it up again? Did it have affection for me, or did the gusts try to test the depth of my "cleanliness"? The last proved not sufficient for me to pick the paper up again.

Connie at hospital with living color in her cheeks—so she's over with it.

Sunday, October 2

Leaves hang tight to our trees and Central Park alight at night is beautiful. Yesterday being a religious holiday for Jews, Joan and Irv went to Temple uptown, took Steffie and then, as per tradition, met with dozens of deafies—Jewish mostly—in Central Park Zoo at the pool for seals. This is an old and quaint tradition—after worship they show off their children to each other.

We picked up Cynthia [176] and had a hamburger and coffee at a 6th Avenue steak joint. Last day of our street art show, and the kids under twelve at their stands were a real joy.

Heard Murrow on the air, who was brave in his attack on State Department pressure on networks, re Khrushchev and Castro, and praised Daly of A.B.C. for slapping down the government interference with the mass media. But Ed's in trouble. He has allowed Paley to put him on ice and then let the ice freeze him.

Saw many girls in tight pants. Want *Life* to run pictures of such females from Front and Fanny Views. This may act

[176] Cynthia Beer, cousin, teacher at City and Country School.

as taste persuader for some whose rears were not built for molded trousers—except in cultures where Rubens' fat women are the vogue.

Monday, October 3

My fast and true friend Russell is dead. He was precious to me—one of the few who deeply influenced my attitudes and desires. Unique among men who influenced our government and banks and much of our spiritual folkway, he was a public character in service but led a private life. I loved him dearly, and my cheer today came when Henry Alexander took time off to call me up to give solace for the death of R. L.

Tuesday, October 4

A mixed day. Up to R. L.'s church for ceremony. Not since Heywood's death have I wept—and why I was ashamed of tears is less than clear. I was a true alien—having never been in touch with Christ, the Holy Ghost or any God. R. L. was a believer, and although we often talked of the mystery of birth and death, we never tried to evangelize each other.

Then to hospital to chat with Connie. As a result must ask Penelope to get me scientific data on possible post-operation, post-hypnotic effects on pain from operations.

Wednesday, October 5

Life moves fast. A letter from Oak Ridge about our one-shot corn experiment. They wrote me:

I have received your letter of September 20, 1960, relative to planting our Atom-Blasted Seeds. Your letter interested me greatly because of the fact that you seemed to be disappointed. Let me remind you, however, that it is not always the gigantic plant that might prove to be beneficial to man. In Sweden barley has been produced which is really a runt compared to the average barley, yet, the Swedes have found that the wind does not blow the plant down; it takes about ½ as much nourishment from the soil; the yield of grain is greater; and when the harvesting is done, the straw is so short that it can be plowed under for the next planting. I would be very much inclined to think from reading your very short letter that you are not looking for the correct things and are expecting giants from these seeds rather than evaluating what you have. Our company is trying to teach people that hereditary characteristics of a plant can be changed this way and we are at the same time trying to teach people that no matter what the change may be, there is a great possibility that many important mutations will be found if people do not become discouraged and will keep looking. Your letter interests me because somewhere along the line *we* have failed to teach you that not all worthwhile mutations are giants. It is quite possible that the seeds from the plants you grew this year, if saved and planted through two or three generations, could result in something very much worthwhile. I am writing this letter to encourage you not to give up. In fact your small plants should encourage you and get you to realize that atomic energy has done something to those seeds or they wouldn't have grown as you described them.

To which I replied:

I am not at all discouraged.
I am too much of an amateur scientist to ever think in terms of encouragement or discouragement.

No lunch and didn't miss it, what with morning coffee and afternoon iced coffee. Connie feeling better in an ungracious hospital—no daily paper until noon and no service of lunch or dinner for guests. Don't doctors ever get sick and thus learn about the will to recovery?

Started a young lawyer on book on Fair Trial. Worked with Catholic friends on issuance of statement on separation of church and state.

Wonderful case of a professor who brought back posters from Russia—held up at customs. To see the posters in Moscow is O.K., but use or display here is deemed dangerous. Surely if we can be subverted by a colored poster, we should resign from the human race.

Leaves turning brown in the Square.

Thursday, October 6

Visited with Cass on Catholic laymen statement concerning church and state. By aiding clarification we now can end the confusion about the Catholic position on Birth Control.

Called on to build an equitable offense to Cuba's theft of copyrighted material—ordered from U.S. citizens, and printed but not paid for. No use suing in Cuba—any more than in Russia. Maybe we might grab Cuban government assets in U.S.—since Castro took over the magazines and papers of the Cuban people.

The show at the U.N. is nearly over. Man can't have, it seems, thoughtful debate and a show (with Castro and other actors) at the same time.

Read Fabricant's *13 Famous Patients*—from Freud's cancer and Joyce's blindness to Darrow's mastoid. It carries new perspectives on the fatal periods in which each of us lives. A decade or two later Proust would not have had to spend his last years in bed, or George Gershwin die of a brain infirmity. Good exciting material for TV—if sadism and breasts did not appear as main ingredients for that medium.

Friday, October 7

Lunch at Ford. Invited to discuss with Pincus *et al.* projects dealing with The Law and more particularly a project including Law teachers, students and practicing members of the profession. I wish these foundations realized that not all projects must be vast, organized and needful of large sums of money. I'd like to run twenty projects on the Law—for an average of $10,000 each. But bigness in the White House and at the State Department and the Chase Bank and Ford all have the same corruption. In Washington recently the State Department sneered at a South American project because it involved only one little million dollars—and a loan, not just a gift, which makes it totally unforgivable. At the Pentagon they tell me: wait a few years. We will develop your idea into a $50 million dollar project, and then you will get it accepted. Big business and government and unions will not admit that life is turned by trifles, by tidbits, and that it contains very few big ideas or big moments.

Off on a minor rampage. All criminal cases should be titled "People or State of New York in the interest of John Doe." No longer should we say, "People against." This change of vernacular may help to emphasize the problem of reorientation of antisocial people. This is the attitude of children's courts since the days of Ben Lindsay in Colorado forty or fifty years ago. Thus might we reject the futile concept of revenge and replace it by reform.

Saturday and Sunday, October 8 and 9

Maggie hears a bluejay crying for rain—and still loafing here before going south. What a great month October is in New York.

To the Plaza for breakfast with Cross, the writer on books in from Milwaukee. No idle chatterer. Never once did we talk: did you like this book? Did you read that book? All such sketchy narrative conversation bores me and now reminds me of the Nixon-Kennedy TV talks—which are so sketchy that no one can conclude what either thinks of Cuba, or Khrushchev, or education. One of these items might have merit for a two-hour debate. As it is, the shows are judged not as to stands on issues—but on the terms of any contest in the field of sport.

Stopped at Zenith, had audiometer test and do not yet need an ear aid.

To office where Penelope calls up to tell me we have two-thirds of the world's TV sets and suggests we should use TV as a weapon; so I throw in the idea that we could debilitate all nations by giving them our fifty million sets. That would make them flabby and reduce their ambitions for things of the mind, and get them to waste their economy on chrome plate and packagings.

Lawyers are not so placid. At least not compared to architects and builders who only recently are allowing plastics to be used for fire safety structures. With the bar—and all professions—those who learned from the outdated books and facts naturally resent doing mayhem to their own past in which they have such a great investment.

Happy the Pirates won—no more than being for the underdog. Started to read *The Last of the Just,* a forceful epic. At night saw Susskind made a fool of by Khrushchev. I guess in return for freedom of the air we must suffer Susskind—but not necessary to suffer him gladly. K. never will have easier meat to chop up. S. is, as Maggie says, "hubristic"—has no humility and is conceited. He asked few questions and all were silly—falling like a babe into K.'s fatherly arms.

221

Tuesday, October 11

Finished looking over Gustav Meyer's *History of Bigotry,* which I read when it was first written. Sober book and should be read by Adam Clayton Powell who talked loud and stern racism at the Kennedy Civil Rights Convention at Park-Sheraton in evening. All the Big were there—E. R., Oscar Chapman, Hubert H. in great form. It's a good idea, although the hundreds there were, as usual, already converted. The value exists, nevertheless, because when President Kennedy (and he's in, for Gallup says it's 50-50, which means, after taking into account his consistent 2 per cent anti-Democrat error, 52-48) then finds a dozen desires—minimum wage, farm bill—and so forth—this meeting will deepen his commitments to move fast and soon in the civil rights area.

Wednesday, October 12

Parade ties up the city. I'll beg once more that the Mall in Central Park be set up for all parades. Of course, the parading show-offs will object because the audiences in the Park would be much smaller and, hence, disappointing. But now parades possess a captive audience of thousands who only want to cross an avenue.

For late breakfast with Harold [177] and suggested Susskind might well explain his ignorance of the phony commercial on his K. show although he should have known all about it.

To Kennedy convention—all thrilled by Mort Sahl, one of our few political satirists. I wonder if Kennedy and Nixon each realizes that whoever is elected has only a hundred days

[177] Harold Stern, attorney.

to ride the big, and maybe only, wave for adoption of their programs.

Home—read Jefferson autobiography which I have missed. Watched end of World Series baseball and tight asleep with the Goldies arriving for dinner.

Thursday, October 13

After listening to campaign oratory about the Founding Fathers and the Constitution, I think we err by not pointing up the errors of these great men. Only thus does man reach the true concept of progress and change. Prior images of perfection point only to backsliding and despair. In Jefferson's diary, written at seventy-seven, I read much about possible, eventual freedom of black people but with an assurance of inevitable and perpetual white superiority. In fact, he approves using a market figure to value Negroes in pounds—this before the Revolution and after. On Criminal law, he favors reduction of capital punishment from one hundred crimes to two—murder and treason. He's for hard labor but not in public—but favors solitary confinement on the basis of a report from Lyon, France. But he put all of the Virginia laws into fewer than one hundred pages—much as Scandinavian cultures have eliminated the legalistic "aforesaids." His observation on a seven-year term for president should be taught in the schools since it was in the Constitution until the next to last day. Also, he knew it was the function of a "good judge to enlarge his jurisdiction." Page Felix F.[178] to the contrary.

On the basis of the two views, we could say to our people: see where we started and how we have improved *even* on Jefferson, Madison, Adams and Franklin.

[178] Supreme Court Justice Frankfurter.

Started to reread Bryce's *American Commonwealth*. This and de Tocqueville should be compulsory in schools and colleges.

Friday, October 14

Last night, Sacco-Vanzetti play was impressive. Unfortunately, it will not be treated as a work of art but rather as an appetizer for propagandists—most of whom were late-comers in the great S.-V. legal defense carried on by Brut Ehrmann and Mr. Thompson of Boston. As with all great cases played up in the press, a bevy of lawyers attached themselves to the cause. The most amusing item I recall was about Art Hayes who, in his book on his career, carried a picture and tale of his battle against Frank Hague—this, even though Art had sued Hague and lost, and had had nothing to do with the final body blow inflicted on "I'm the Law" Hague by the Supreme Court. I never could understand this because Art was a magnificent defender of the faith, who had enough victories of his own not to horn in on those of others.

To Dr. Rosen for a deafness check-up. Then to Connie at hospital. She is in top form and goes home tomorrow. Then to my dictatings. To lunch with Jess Morgan [178a] of Hollywood, discussing public underwritings of TV producers; to John and Jane Gunther; to Fred Nathans' [178b] for cocktails; out to dinner with Paula and Alan at Sokol, the Free Czech place.

Wrote the presidential candidates that divulgence creates havoc. Even between those in love, there are areas of needed reserve. Between those who do not trust each other, disclosures of future tactics are dangerous. With Jack K. saying

[178a] Financial advisor in movie field.
[178b] Law partner.

he would not defend the islands off China, I should imagine that Chiang may withdraw if K. is elected. Too much talk. Why show our hand to an enemy—one beneath the area of trust?

Saturday, October 15

Maggie scolds me because I did not convert her to the joys of a shower years ago. Yesterday we rediscovered one of New York's great and unknown restaurants—Sokol—where, after Czech food (potato soup and very crisp roast duck) you can walk over the sill and play or watch basketball. Fabulous Goodie [179] arrives from London—he of Chestertonian build, Walter Pater rhythm of sentence and Chesterfieldian courtesy.

Wrote letter to Dick and Jack,[180] as follows:

MY DEAR MR. PRESIDENT

  or

DEAR JACK AND DICK

I am disturbed for the sake of our Republic at the subtle but dangerous shift from political discussion into a format of a Quiz Show. I wonder if you could not agree on a *joint* statement that goes to all future questions of basic diplomacy with the arch enemy of our society—Communist Colonialism.

When the Constitution of the United States was drafted in 1787, the second resolution adopted provided that all discussion shall be *secret* so that the delegates could more readily change their minds. In fact, there would have been no Constitution agreed upon if our 100 weekly gazettes had had access to the debates. As you know, Ben Franklin was accompanied by younger delegates to his tavern every night so as to make certain that he would not blab the day's proceedings.

179 Arnold Goodman, solicitor.
180 Richard Nixon and John F. Kennedy.

Even between people in tender love, there must be areas of reserve; no spouse dares tell the other all of his or her thoughts. All the more reason why, with people we do not trust, it seems to me perilous to have the present game proceed so that the public will get some temporary pleasure in watching the matching of wits rather than permit our nation and the next president to use uncommitted and undisclosed moves of diplomacy. Whether we give up certain islands or not is remote from the issue I am writing to you about. My concern is that the matter should not be discussed in terms of strategy in a public debate. Neither of you would ask for a plebiscite on such a matter, which may involve strategy always subjected to other considerations raised by history at the moment when a decision is called for.

I must be frank in saying that the questions from the reporters at your debates are bound to disturb the next president. None of the questions go to philosophy of government or the destiny of our Republic. In the main, they are the usual dirty quiz or panel questions, not to get the truth, but to catch one or the other of you in an inconsistency.

I understand that pressure which made both of you submit to this inadequate exhibition. Might you not now issue a joint formal statement that makes clear that there are areas which should not be divulged or exposed in advance to the general public, much less to our opponents, and, at most, should be addressed to allies who can be trusted? I am fearful that the American public is engaged in a game to discover who can best needle the other, who is best at repartee and who has many arts—none of which necessarily go to the question of stature for the Chief Magistrate of our nation.

With non-partisan good will, I address this letter. Our Republic is in dire trouble. If I can help in the direction of such a joint declaration of statesmanship, do not hesitate to call on me.

Yours,

Four-hour lunch with Dick [181] and Goodie. Arrived hour early (calendar broke) and just contemplated and talked to

[181] Richard Ader, law partner.

waiters—one who is an iced coffee bummer, as I am, another who went back to Wien after years. In evening, to *Harvest* and *Carnival in Flanders,* two old pictures which I had seen and forgotten, but which delighted me. Surely, too many dollars spoil pictures, actors and producers.

Sunday, October 16

Maggie fixed breakfast—waffles, berries and the works—and feels proud at her house-wifery which I deny her only at breakfast. Otherwise I like being waited on, spoiled and even being domineered.

As Disraeli or someone of the English Cabinet said, "With words we govern men." And so the great *Times* has inched up a trifle on its most difficult chore—admission of error of leadership in Cuba. This day, October 16, 1960, it said, "Castro has NOW ... made Cuba a Communist satellite." How difficult it is for man to admit error. The *Times* is rich, the greatest of all papers, but still not secure enough to write, "We were wrong. Cuba was Communist when Stuart Novins so reported on TV—maybe before, but we were not wise or smart enough to realize it. We apologize."

Mort [182] and his bride-to-be for breakfast, then to Bessies' to see Connie at home, then to party at Lena L.'s. In between, good talk with Boorstin, an historian of United States folkways. Lena sweetly suggested publishers give parties to authors when a first book comes out. So Lena gives us a party for our 20th or 21st.

[182] Morton Goldberg, lawyer.

Tuesday, October 18

Wrote Frank Hogan about horrors of TV interviews of indicted money winners. Horror is that these persons are only charged—no proof of guilt—and we have an indecent show which the Bar Associations should and could stop tomorrow morning, at the latest, if they cared about fair trial, or as we call it, due process.

Wednesday, October 19

Joan and Irv's wedding anniversary. All set for one of those celebration dinners. And then I learn that Arlene, the precious maid, is at a hospital—second degree burns. Once more the myth is exploded that when children grow up, marry and fly the coop, all troubles are at an end for parents. Nothing to it. What with baby-sitting and the like for Maggie, the candidates for consideration and concern have increased manifold.

Lunch with E. S., who relates exciting news from the *New York Times*—publication of the New York edition in Paris for all of Europe.

Excited about an English-built yawl for sale at Norwalk. The choice is between this and the reverse sheer Constellation. The latter on any rational test gets higher marks. But— and it's an important but—I cannot fall in love with the line of the Constellation. Somehow man assumes that sail areas and location of galley, and even speed, are more real than the curve of a bow. So I'll see the Norwalk vessel.

Home for dinner. Finished Steve Allen's book—not well written, quite full of guilts for mankind, confused as to his religion, but a writing of high value because of his status which can persuade the unpersuaded—in fact, those who seldom read words in a hard cover.

Thursday, October 20

Up early with a mind choked with problems—none of my own or my close ones, but of clients. Fixed coffee and juice and read papers, exchanging with Maggie tidbits from *Times* and *Tribune*. Noted a tiny fly in my honey jar. Have seen no fly in the apartment this fall but this shrewd beast came out from some crack in some room and went for the honey. What is it—smell? I doubt if insects have a keen sense of smell. If not, what wave carried between the honey and the fly?

To Town House for breakfast with Hiram. He's delighted with the reviews of *Touch Wood*, and I'm no longer embarrassed for fear he might unconsciously resent me for sticking his chin out and taking it for publication. Amused that reviews, though kind, still beg for more professional secrets. So wrote Duffus of *Times*, "Come to me on your next divorce and I'll put all the lugubrious dirt in the next edition of *T.W.*"

Letters pour in on *T.W.* Of course only friendly feelings elicit such letters. Not like those I get after a radio talk—then it's often anonymous, and "You dirty Kike—you Communist—go back where you came from."

Friday, October 21

Last evening's meeting stays in mind—as full of good will and waste. Monroney, Fulbright and Averell made brief talks to a group of about thirty—all of whom know the score and are committed to the Democratic Party. Benton brought along a songster. But it was all incestuous—the Democrats talk only to Democrats. Governor Lehman made a wise comment: why don't the Midwest senators come to New York—other than to raise money every four years? I explain my theory of the misfortune of a capital out of the streams of culture, traffic and commerce. No one goes to Washington except to get something or to block something. Our rulers in Washington see too little of normal folk. I'll bet there are one hundred rich men and women who had never heard the honorable senators, who would have paid $1,000 apiece just to go to Ave's home, see the beauty of his art, listen and brag about it to friends. A silly gathering of the noble and converted. I only enjoy meeting those I disagree with.

Exciting combat and hence helpful talk with David Owen and Hans Singer [183] about my paper on Year 2000. Surely responsible officials must view truth in terms of its effect. So our proof that the gap in living standard won't start to close between us and India, for example, until the year 2017, causes many to think the idea will create despair rather than a big new plan and approach. This retarding attitude of many is not unlike that surrounding the introduction of the spinning wheel in Lancashire.

No more Hong Kong shoes—down to my last pair from 1955, so will buy me a half dozen new ones. No laces, all alike, all interchangeable.

In evening to Pat Delhi's book store for party for our two books. Rather good fun—showing off in moderation. Home early and watched what I hope will be the last Nixon-Kennedy Quiz Show. Once more my candidate sheds diplomacy and talks about Cuba. Maggie sagely suggests this will not be repeated in 1964. Will Kennedy or Nixon, as President running for reelection, go on a show with an opposition candidate?

A card from Rabbi in Natchez, who reminds me that at the time of Berlin crisis I told Bill Fulbright that it was a cover-

[183] Both of U.N. Secretariat.

up—a diversionary tactic for getting a base in South America. And the Communists have done it.

Sunday, October 23

Woke up and told Maggie I hope I'll fall in love today. She as jealous as a bride—but knew I was to see a yawl at Norwalk and I have long been wanting to buy a new boat. But I must fall in love before owning. "Falling" is well used as a concept with boats but not too valid with women—or even wives. Then there is also a chance of rising in love. On the way up to the Norwalk Yacht Club in the Schwartz' buggy, I remarked, "Maybe I'll buy my next-to-last boat today." Maggie smiled at the "next to last" but I explained no one should ever talk or think of "last." I have heard people say, "I'll never see the Taj again, or walk across Switzerland, or fly to Africa." Who knows? Kinsey found males having children at over 80. Although there are exceptions to the ban against the phrase "never again," on the whole it's a defeatist concept—even to fend off mistakes.

I didn't fall in love with a beautifully-built British boat. And like unlove or love, it is indefinable.

Home—nap, read papers and then to the Garden to hear my favorite organist Gladys Goodings, and watch the Rangers get licked. I missed seeing the fine figure of Reed Kilpatrick.

Monday, October 24

Law duties. Lunch with George Hecht and Kendig of Doubleday Book Shops. Alan and I suggested two programs. Raise stature of managers of stores. Each to recommend, by window placard or otherwise, the books he liked each week.

231

These book store managers should be the literary guides for their customers rather than let a Fadiman select, by predigested choice, book club selections. What a wonderful revolution if, in a decade, the public looks up with esteem to their book store managers. George saw no infirmity. The other project: we are to draft a window sign, "Have you books you are not likely to reread? Why not donate them to the hospital or prison of your choice? Doubleday will deliver if you bring in. If sets or quantities, we will pick up and deliver. And you can take a tax deduction for a fair valuation."

This can do mighty things. A full shelf retards purchases. An empty hole in a shelf invites purchase of more.

For dinner with Leon Lowenstein at Coach Club, a new club organized, I suspect, to get rid of a valuable piece of property. The waitresses in tights, and I mean tight tights. Tasteless—but the food is tasty. Home, and then to Eden Roc for party of a hundred stage people for Radie Harris, a writer of tidbits who is never cruel and, in fact, helps to counteract the ordinary run of peephole writers. Lucky—was seated between Margalo and Smith.[184] Home and to bed. Like old times—light out after 2 A.M.

Tuesday, October 25

Picked up stranger in cab to office, a tin man from Continental Can. Talk went to our survey, that if the rest of the world attains one-fourth of our living standard, there is no estimate that shows enough tin for the people of the planet. So what? We go to synthetics, and then realize there ain't enough power in sight—gas, oil, uranium or water. So what? We go to old Sol—whose energy is everlasting.

To Woodmere to speak to 450 ladies of The National Coun-

[184] Ethel Smith, musician.

cil of Jewish Women at authors' book luncheon. Other speakers humorous and engaging. Then my vanity was fed by forty requests for signatures in books. Surely, I liked it. One good looking gal stumped me for an inscription. Made her wait and then wrote, "Dr. Freud inhibited me." She blushed and loved it.

In the evening to see a horror picture, *The Alamo*. What a distortion of history! To Hollywood, history can never be subtle. Left at the halfway mark.

Home to bed, after the Card [185] girls from down the hall, whom I met in the elevator, came in for a drink. 2 Fifth Avenue is getting to be like our old home on 11th Street—part of a little intimate village.

Thursday, October 27

Cynth in for coffee last night—unexpected and unannounced, which is the better fashion for unorganized sociability. She's a born teacher—hence a welcome visitor.

Lunch with a sailing gent from England, whom I fell for since he owns a Dutch pilot sloop. Wants little company on board, and we swapped pictures of vessels, and attitudes about the never-satisfied boat ownership of all sensible folk.

Dictated on machine—filling two tapes on Law Series volume on censorship cases. I usually do not relish reliving any of my past, but enjoyed these memories—like roses in December.

Letter from our Marie whom we love and miss much and often. To dinner at home with Connie and Margalo. John Martin [186] of Kennedy train drops in later. Wise and able person.

[185] Mary Card, teacher at City and Country School, and sister.
[186] John Bartlow Martin, writer, and ambassador.

Decided to give my Joyce collection, or at least a part, to U. of Texas. A little regret, but not too much, to part with *Ulysses* inscribed by Joyce, with flattering words about my legalization of his major work—a work stolen from him until our test case. Never a penny of royalty before 1935 but then his first check was over $20,000—enough for wine and an eye operation.

Friday, October 28

Sent my New Year Resolution on Hopes to *Variety* as follows:

VARIETY

Here are a few hopes for the coming years. Some are old, some new.

1. Our Republic should start at once an investigation as to the advantages and dangers of the facsimile printing of newspapers throughout the United States. Unless we are farsighted, this exciting process will soon be so inexpensive as to produce a vast increase of overwhelming orthodoxy.

2. I am still bewildered that, in the recent census, there was no question dealing with theatre, books, magazines, movies or other culture media. Why were the questions directed only toward toilets, running water, TV sets, deep freeze and the like? In January 1961, a joint committee of all culture groups should prepare for the next census. Or is the mind less important than material possessions?

3. The market place of theatre, movies and TV is peculiarly dirty since lawyers act as agents and agents act as lawyers. Surely if we are concerned with conflicts of interests of officials in our government, we should be even more disturbed by the condoned conflicts of interest in the entertainment field.

4. For about 80 years, newsprint has entered our shores free

of tariff, but there is a tariff on book and magazine paper. In 1961 I hope to get the answer to this unconscionable and irrational discrimination.

5. I am delighted that at long last publishers and writers of music have been alerted to the vast tax savings that can be honorably procured in that portion of our culture. Holders of patents are tax preferred compared to holders of copyrights. This discrimination against the mind of man can be easily eliminated by the leaders of our culture. Senator Kennedy stated:

> I think we can do better than that, if only by alleviating the unfair tax burden borne by writers, painters, and other creative artists. They may exist on small incomes for years to perfect their skills, and then be plundered by the Treasury in a single year of plenty.

6. Russia has threatened to join the Copyright Convention in order to prevent the translation into English of its increasingly great list of technical scientific books. Our nation and the leaders of the publishing business must be ready for this attack on the free market place of thought by the Communist dictators.

7. One of the great burdens on much of the entertainment in our land results from the historically explainable pursuit of unions to procure spread of employment and pensions for the aged through burdening industry with excessive payrolls, which in turn raise prices and reduce audiences. I trust that in 1961 some leadership will develop to call a Convention of all these unions so as to take care of the proper objectives of workers by machinery other than by boondoggling—which raises costs and reduces audiences.

Saturday, October 29

Heard from Jeff Sparks [187] and our law office is off on another bright adventure. At our next monthly meeting a

[187] UN head of TV and radio.

UN attorney from Belgium will be the guest. The following months lawyers from Greece, Liberia, Japan.

I despise dinners as I do the bellyache, and funerals as I do death. I avoid both. Only from small luncheons, and under rare setups, does anything of value develop. For years our office luncheons have been the dullest of the dull—pedestrian and conventional. They diminished good will—whatever that may mean. Basically my objection lies in the fact that if a man has something worth saying, he will probably write it and then I can read it. Only rarely I think is the feel of a personality enriching. But now we go beyond our prior exchange of lawyers with a British solicitor's office—for now we will be able, without speeches, and only by Q. and A., to get knowledge not readily available. For example, I'd like to ask the effect of part of the Senate in Belgium being selected other than by direct vote. Also, the effect of the government paying part of clergy salaries. Catholicism is dominant, but they even pay for Jewish rabbis—similar to Trujillo who has aroused great Catholic animosity by building houses of worship for all religions.

To lunch with Poppy Cannon [188] who is off to Nigeria. I envy her. Have only been in a few west coast African towns, and then during the war. All quite different from Morocco, Egypt, Lebanon and Israel where we traveled at various times. I suggest that wherever the British have been, the chances for self-government are far above where the British have not been.

Sunday, October 30

Plane to Providence to ACLU branch meeting. Panel discussion on Separation of Church and State with an eminent

[188] Writer, Mrs. Walter White.

Catholic, in frock, talking with good will. The audience was suspicious and alarmed to learn that that Church was not monolithic. I followed, at a dinner, to tell of Catholic Index, which, I'm making book, will be abandoned at the Ecumenical Congress in Rome in 1962. Also on birth control and break-up of marriage where Church is totally misunderstood. There ain't no one Catholic Church on most issues—it's only monolithic because non-Catholics make it so by so believing.

November

Thursday, November 3

Modern magic. Jet to Birmingham, car at airport and on our way through good uncluttered Alabama roads to Union-town. An odd emotional experience. Seventy years ago I left this town, still of 1,700 heads. To Mayor's office where two gracious bureaucrats were waiting. They gave me pictures of my birth home and then, as is normal, showed me list of Jews buried in cemetery. Not interested at all in Jewish or any cemeteries—not even concerned with cremation. Enough of an excitement just living until I die. I handled the courtesy of the Mayor's staff on this score without offense, I trust.

Dropped in on Economy Store run by Abe Cohen—the only Jew, he told me, in the town. Here my father and his brother had their store, the bank—their world where, as two immigrants shipped with labels around their necks addressed to Uniontown, Ala., they landed from Pilsen, Bohemia, not long after our Civil War—with, I assume, a spoon and a cup. Having no memory back to 1890, and never having heard my parents tell tales of our days in the South, I approached this town with something near remoteness—not quite as part of me. The Mayor's wife, a blue-eyed beauty, met us and guided us around. The house where I was born stands sturdy with a few changes, but is still quite elegant. Then to visit Carl Morgan whose father worked for my father, and who was named after my father sixty-eight years ago. Quite touched. He's a sturdy, gusty, affirmative person. He told tales of his father's loyalty and affection for Carl Ernst. The name Carl has gone on for three generations in the Morgan clan. All folk were kindly and warm, but I still feel as if I were hearing of another person, another family. Nearly a feeling of loneliness—at least aloneness—since I have no known heritage and I'd much like one.

The trees were beautiful—those great oaks, handsomer by far than the linden at our Square which has lost its leaves. Here the foliage is just going rust-red. I wish I could have been hypnotized, and thus picked up bits of memory of my earliest two years, 1888 to 1890.

Alabama has beauty: the roadsides are cut back with charm, the folkway quite different—but of course we compromised when we went to dinner near the Plaza Motel, outside of Demopolis, and entered under a sign, "Whites Only." What the South suffered from is the absence of the Wycliffe Bible with its 1684 introduction, "Of, For and By the People." That religious precept was a wealth-maker, and though Calvinism had less hell fire in the North than the Methodist-Baptist culture in the South, still New England's gods made wealth. New England churches were equally stern and full of hell fire, but Satan frowning on laziness, made for industry. Of course the climate helped the North mightily.

Said goodbye to Uniontown—as if I were a stranger—bemused, delighted but untouched by sentiment or sentimentality. Fate. What would I have been if the family had remained in the South?

Friday and Saturday, November 4 and 5

Good motel last night and red carpet when we mentioned Carl Morgan. What low-cost living where no fending against zero cold and no need for insulation, heating and fur coats.

Drove to beautiful Mobile. Then drove on with Mal and Ike [189] to Bellingrath Gardens—a rare and beautiful monument of recent creation, with income from gate receipts paid to Negro institutions. These gardens can be sustained by man so as to endure longer even than the Taj Mahal. Then on to shore drive to Broadwater Beach—a truly lovely inn built in motel style.

To Royal Orleans hotel in the center of the Greenwich Village area of New Orleans. Beautiful hotel, but architects only live on squared paper. No space for toilet articles in bathrooms and a light unfit to read by.

For lunch Peter [190] invited a half dozen or so young New Orleans barristers. Good talk as to trends of the bar. But this city is running scared on the segregation issue. No one seems to think in span of years, and hence the conflicts are of the moment, which always invites dogmatism and reduction of good will. Above all, I'm sure here there is no leadership. There is not even an elder statesman in sight, a Baruch, Hoover or Lehman—men beyond the age of being bribed by

[189] Lowenburgs, cousins from New Orleans.
[190] Peter Beer, cousin, lawyer.

life. I do believe this absence of leadership is more unfortunate even than the color conflict.

The lawyers were keen and of attitudes that I would enjoy retaining or working with.

Maggie with Ret [191] to Galatoire's for Oysters Rockefeller for lunch—and then we dined in private room at Antoine's with Maggie's entire family. Meanwhile she visited with Ida Friend, my idea of a great southern leader—but now in her nineties and for Nixon, even though she had been State Democratic Committee woman for many years.

Weather perfect and I'm tempted to emigrate from Manhattan. What a challenge New Orleans presents!

Sunday, November 6

No one I've met seems to realize that the great destiny of our Republic is to act as leader and bridge in the major conflict of the next century, the Color Problem. Our Republic and ours alone can lead this struggle. No other nation, beating the color problem internally, will be able to pose as an example of world leadership. Only in our nation is the conflict of such substantial size that our success can make us great throughout the world.

Up on roof of hotel for good sun bath and my traditional iced coffee. For lunch out at the lake with Jimmy [192] and Ret for New Orleans fish food, and then to visit Maggie's former friends, all over eighty. Telephone lines kept busy as result of story in *Times-Picayune* about Maggie's arrival and books.

Second thoughts: the French Quarter is not Greenwich Village except that both areas accommodate the creative and unorthodox, and both capitalize on honky-tonks "for visitors

[191] Ret Beer, cousin.
[192] Jimmy Beer, cousin.

only"—but this old area here has maintained its history, its antiquity and the physical evidences of a great tradition.

Third thoughts: this city has jitters—the enemy of leadership. Telephone calls as result of newspaper interview show that everyone is troubled and does little more than reflect calamities, as if by memory. This repetition seems to take the place of constructive action. One anonymous call: "Go back where you came from!" I said "O.K. I'm from Alabama." Silence—message ended with an angry click.

For dinner with Maggie's younger cousins—dedicated good citizens. Home early and to bed after watching TV—once more I note sad concentration of programming in New York and Hollywood. There must be creative folk here, but the economics of bigness—and particularly network bigness—make it look as if there were in all of New Orleans no boy with a fiddle or girl with a song in her heart. Must all talent be shunted to Manhattan, to be sterilized in that city where people scarcely remember that our nation extends west of the Hudson?

Monday, November 7

In cab to airport, on way to Houston for lunch, a much bewildered lady mentions Washington Square and tells us that she lives at Washington Place; and when Maggie says we live at 2 Fifth, the lady with elation says, "That's where Morris Ernst lives." Such is the notoriety of Ed Murrow's "Person to Person."

One more beautiful day as we ate a Texas breakfast on plane; with gusto we take in juice, sausage, eggs, grits, coffee and various rolls. No thin-blooded folk down this way.

Just read research on Uniontown and learn population in

1890 was 854, rising in 1910 to 1834, and now about 1800. But it has four banks with a white population of only 650. When my folks lived there the number of homes could not have exceeded 150 or 200.

In Houston we stepped right into the Lyndon Johnson campaign headquarters. He spoke like an old time campaigner —a mixture of wise statesmanship and tear-jerking. The feeling here runs strong, and the splits are not only on wealth, but between partners and in families. Lunch with Bill Taylor [193] and his clients whom we served on a big matter last year.

Then to Ben Levy [194] to sit with lawyers concerned with civil liberties matters and more particularly, police brutality. More dedicated men and women I never have met—but too much, at least for me, of a feeling of hopelessness.

On to plane to Austin (and University of Texas) where gaily met by Otis Singletary and Frances Hudspeth. [195] Cleaned up, and then a great steak at Headliners Club. Much impressed by these folk and the obvious high adventure which President Harry Ransom has instilled in them.

Weary and to bed, but good to be in Texas—a state on the march, where men can try and fail and try again. The opportunity to try after failure is a great wealth-maker. And here there is leadership of all sorts—good or bad—but leadership! In New Orleans I found despair and a complaining society. Texas isn't really South. It's West.

Tuesday, November 8

Texas I like. No more road signs: "Where will you spend Eternity." Cremation is legal, and hotel is not elegant. So

[193] Texas attorney.
[194] American Civil Liberties Union lawyer, Houston.
[195] Both of University of Texas.

Maggie takes out her little soft pillow without which she seldom travels.

Professor Silber of Philosophy Department turns over his class—about one hundred boys and girls. Talked on relation of the open market place of thought as compared to Plato's fears of ideas, protection of society from evil. Questions really acute and tough—kept me on my toes.

Then to lunch with Otis, Professor Silber and an expert on South America. Learned that our Information Service Library in Argentina is in richest street—instead of, for same money, having three or four offices where masses of inquisitive people are living. Same old State Department ignorance of folkways. I'd like a Foreign Office of men with blue jeans instead of striped pants.

After lunch to a group of about thirty students—just batting ideas around. After two hours still pleasurable and so to coffee shop. Joined by professors of English Department.

To dinner at Headliners Club. Watched returns until midnight. Truly close vote. This will be wholesome for advisors to Kennedy. Few people can stand a landslide. On and off during the night woke up to get returns. This, even though close, may be accepted as a repudiation of the Do-Nothing Ike attitudes toward government. I hope so, even though the Democratic Party did little to help. It always, from 1952, treated Ike as the sacred, tired, but lovable old uncle who visits us once in a while.

Had a nice dream. There was only one tree left in the world. All of the talk of need of trees for pulp or to catch rain disappeared. This tree was treated like a shrine and all of mankind went on a crusade to discover how to preserve it forever. Why? Only because of its beauty and not because of rarity. Tried to get meaning of the dream. No luck.

Wednesday, November 9

Busy full and varied day. Lectured at Professor Ayers' course on social science and anthropology—giving random examples of the uses of this science to lawyers. Good class, tough questioners.

Then to lunch with local ACLU—with masochists who enjoy defeats.

Then to a self-organized student group for three hours of random questions: censorship, sexual mores, foreign aid, competition with authoritarian—supposedly superior—use of uneducated labor force.

Then to dinner with student group selected by the President. Superior minds and attractive people. This lasted until midnight although girls, treated as less than mature, had to be back in dorms by eleven o'clock. Some rebellion under way to such supervision as shown by cheating; no effect on sexual patterns (my questions on campus lead to a figure lower than in other segregated women's colleges—60 per cent virgin at time of graduation). Maggie and I both had great evening.

To lunch room for a snack and then to bed—feeling satisfied that this is a great and rare institution. One more day—devoted to law school faculty and freshmen.

Friday, November 11

Off to Dallas and to lunch with a lawyer who has an archaeological bride studying at Harvard. Chatted a moment with Stanley Marcus and looked over his store. Surprised that Nieman-Marcus has a sign on the pilaster at the door—it's a small sign but would the Bank of England have a sign (or does it?).

Interviews by press and radio. To dinner with Lon Tinkle, one of the few good conversationalists I have met. The Dobies [196] are truly entrancing—he looks like a nonsentimental Carl Sandburg. Food at Old Warsaw is worthy of mention in a U.S. Michelin Guide if we ever get one. There we met as book-minded a group as I have ever seen gathered in any city of our land. All concerned with the Book and Author lunch which draws a crowd of over a thousand. Then we went to lavish home of John William Rogers, and talk with one and sundry—all concerned with freedom from government control over the mind of men.

I prefer the mood of Austin to that of Dallas which suffers from a legend that all are rich. Maybe Princeton and Austin are the culture centers of our nation—excelling Harvard and Yale. I do hope that Ransom can keep the college from getting bigger, but Gargantua is a sneaky and insidious enemy of government, unions, business and even culture.

Saturday, November 12

Heavy weather. I doubt if I have ever experienced heavy fog so far inland. Book and Author lunch went off under delightful Lon's chairmanship in great acclaim. Dobie was good for the souls of all—Harnett Kane and Ciardi quipped to the satisfaction of the ladies present, and I tried to bring them back to the dangers of literary censorship—talking about tawdriness of the bulk of our dailies and much of TV. Talked of nonmonolithic Catholic Church.

After the lunch of a thousand, far greater audience than

[196] Frank Dobie, writer.

in New York, to Gilliland's book store where Maggie and I autographed for an hour or so.

To a party at my favorite oil baron, Jake Hamon. One of the best-read gents I have ever talked to in or out of Texas.

Sunday, November 13

Picked up an Avis car and drove through Fort Worth—through dreary undistinguished flatlands to Chandor Gardens. Odd spectacle—not as whimsical or attractive as I would have expected from the mind of man who painted F. D. R. and Churchill. At Mrs. Chandor's, a Dr. White for lunch—a man not only knowledgeable but able to remember and quote from classics in fitting fashion.

Back to what is called by local amateurs Big D., dinner in room and then to Alan Bromberg's lovely home to meet with lawyers and newspaper gentry. Still can't get lowdown on the conventions of wine and women in Texas. In Dallas there is local option by districts of the city—further complicating conclusions. But no one tells me in satisfactory terms where girls who want a roll in the hay meet up with men who are not too resistant to the idea. The Beer Clubs are too sporadic, the regular phoney clubs for drinking are designed for the rich.

Monday, November 14

All day at Southern Methodist University Law School. M. leaves me here to pick up some old Natchez buddies with odd names like Blossom. Lunch with faculty and subdued students; then fifty students at 3 o'clock; coffee break and they put me back to work at 6 o'clock before a hundred embryonic students. Then dinner with Dean Jack Riehm, an exceptionally appreciative lawyer-executive, and a few of his staff at a beautiful club overlooking the city. The Clubs are cynical demonstrations of a State—hypocritical on liquor and thus inducing bottle-buying which means bottle-drinking, for no one leaves half a bottle. But this is for the rich; the poor drink beer or wine at bars.

The Law School is the right size, although it's my guess it excels the University of Texas in Learning but is inferior in hurdling over to Thinking. The students are politically sterile, and this means more than just Republican. They—on a show of hands in several groups—intend to practice in big cities and vote as their fathers do. Worse yet, mothers vote as fathers do. They claim their rebellion is against last decades of liberalism. Nonsense. Their rebellion, they admitted when faculty absent, lies in sexual behavior and, more important, in integration. But on that burning issue they do not talk up to or at the Papas. All good fun; and questions were piercing.

Tuesday, November 15

Back at Southern Methodist University for the morning— a hundred or so students. They asked questions—no lecturing by me. Asked about Galindez but not surprised that he was a U.S. agent. All troubled about Cuba.

Lunch with students and no faculty. Rebellion stirring against Methodist no-drink rules, even though I'm assured that half of Methodist Church congregations do drink hard liquor.

Back to hotel. Frank Schultz [197] picks me up and takes me to Dallas Petroleum Club. Saw him last at Ritz in Paris when

197 Dallas oil engineer.

he was starting his North Africa oil development. We recalled our trip to Cairo around 1952.

Plane to San Francisco—late an hour or so, but though weary, relaxed at mere idea of this unique city. Slept restlessly with M. far away. She flew home.

Wednesday, November 16

A city with its own flavor, San Francisco—gateway to Pacific, to Klondike, to adventure. Outward patterns are polite: autoists yield, pedestrians respect signs at intersections, passengers for trams wait placidly and often long, but away from curb. Little communication between scholars of university and leaders of industry; but the arts have good roots—deep enough to permit growth of unclean beatniks, those young people who are umbilically bound, using beards instead of jack knives and poems instead of guns to show their adolescent hatred of mamas and papas. Saloons like those of Switzerland where respectable working girls can meet boys, chat, drink and not go to bed together the same night.

To Donna and Charlie's for lunch. Tasteful living—even elegant, but sculpture and paintings not of prestige name patterns. Fell in love with a piece, no more than a combination of two big hunks of driftwood. Lawyers at lunch—heated arguments derived from my unalterable idea that victories are sweet and good for man, and that traditional tactics in the battles for decency can always be beaten by inventing new approaches.

Luther Nichols, culture book spirit of the area, picked me up for an afternoon snifter. Item: loud-speaker announcing systems in all hotels and assembly places sound like Donald Duck. Did Disney get his quacking speech from the real duck, or did the inventor of loud-speakers raise ducks and unconsciously imitate them?

Delightful talk with Nichols—mainly about converting retail book store managers into spiritual book guides for their communities.

At seven George Davis [198] picked me up and took me to Berkeley where I talked on censorship, with questions from students. Picked up Koshlands [199] at Trader Vic's after steak with George; then on to Hot Spot where adults acted like children—friendly, noisy and full of booze. All for out-of-towners and less wise than rollicking at Texas Guinan's with Broun thirty years ago.

On the town to bars. Maggie in New York so I looked for the Kit Kat of Lebanon, Chez Vous of Casablanca and all those dives adorned with nude women, like the night clubs of foreign cities which I have never attended, always blaming, in teasing fashion, my noncensorious bride.

Thursday, November 17

A living city, a gateway—not like Lisbon, or Marseilles, but civilized in all aspects.

Slept late after a night of so-called gaiety seeing the town. Pretty silly and not unlike uptowners coming to Greenwich Village to hot spots which we villagers have not yet even entered.

In the morning to visit at law shop of Stanley Weigel, the stout barrister who fought the Regents of California on the teacher-oath issue. The disapproval of his clients has surely been converted into high praise. Then to lunch with lawyer

[198] Attorney.
[199] D. Koshland, business executive, and wife, the former Lucile Heming, active in League of Women Voters.

Berman who is counsel to the lad under charges arising out of unfitness of local police and the disorder of students protesting to House Committee on Un-American Activities. Berman is a wise tactician.

To dinner in Los Angeles with Jess Morgan who kindly arranged a dinner party for me. So I'm finished with my own Adult Education through questions of students—Texas and California decidedly worthwhile.

Friday, November 18

In L.A., which I neither relish nor cherish. It has no form or character and it sprawls without a core or center. It has no commons—the heart of a city—and hence its heartbeat is vague. It lives on the tawdry frame of artificial personalities (blown up by press agents for people who don't think but do envy), hairdos (I love my gals with rumpled hair), vaunted bosoms (too exaggerated for my taste—a real breast need not boast) and men who are so moral they must marry every other girl they go to bed with.

Traveling I pick up odd new or old relationships. Dorothy Gray, beautiful as ever, Marjorie Mayer's daughter, a student at Berkeley, sitting starry-eyed in front row; Myron Cohen, still acting with humility, with whom I exchange admiration.

To Moulin Rouge for Book and Author luncheon. It did real harm to the concept of books. A good writer, such as Uris, says nothing and tries to compete with Steve Allen gags, and then puts on a hoax, suitable for a convention to promote can openers, or trash baskets. One thousand women came to look at writers, and leave with less than if they had gone to a zoo or a one-ring circus. Arlene Francis tells about her teeth and does not even nibble at the world of letters. The audience has a high time, but it's all anti-ideas. It's a TV comic show in the flesh. Richard Armour, a professor, tries to prove he writes to order and for money, with no regard to the possible place of books in our culture. I send Steve Allen notes—or prayers—to please utter a thought; I begged him for an idea. But he spends three-fourths of his time on gags, stooping needlessly to his audience. He talked not only down, but as if the dames were deep in a cave. Then he went to the atomic bomb problem and spoke from the heart.

Disgusted, and rushed out with Cynthia Lindsay without being polite enough to autograph copies of *Touch Wood*. Maybe the Publishers' Council should make a study of the Book and Author lunch racket and help produce a sane format. The food was uneatable, and the program made me sick in the pit of my stomach.

In the evening preferred a session of Moldof's group on St. Francis of Assisi to company of glamor friends. Most interesting—previously unacquainted dozen meet for two hours to wrangle in Talmudic fashion over their impressions of Francis: was it a myth, or did he talk to birds, even to a wolf? did he offer Heaven in the hereafter because he had no knowledge sufficient to bestow bits of Heaven on earth? They talked to the core of our foreign aid program without being aware of it. All earnest—a few leaping minds, but the slow witted and even the illogical helped mold the evening. Then to coffee joint, and had a chance to talk to one of group, Julie Adams, skilled actress and a beauty who nevertheless used her mind.

Saturday, November 19

Loafed in morning and then plane to Phoenix. Soon felt that this city is an infant town in a frontier state. It has no core. One-newspaper town; and taxi drivers, motel employees, merchants and all others I met, cynical of press. Town in heat —in groups—over picture taken by Westinghouse and *Chronicle* TV stations in San Francisco showing the police creation of student disturbance at hearings of House Committee on Un-American Activities. The film is being sold to groups, pressured into schools and, many believe, it is not only onesided but put into circulation corruptly by the House Committee.

Dinner with ACLU group; energetic, devoted, honorable but uninventive and enjoying, a little too much for my taste, being pushed around and harassed by anonymous letter writers and the like. Spoke in auditorium for two hours including questions. Audience was divided, but all went well except for one lad in gallery who started to use Communist tactics, by interrupting other questioners. Mrs. Grailcourt of ACLU spoke better than I had expected and, no doubt, worried those who think all protestors against violation of the committee brand of due process must be Communist.

Sunday, November 20

Inefficiency puts me on a nonjet, so spent nine hours on TWA to New York. Slept, read, and happy to note that this line answered my plea for hooks for Maggie's ever-slipping purses. Also it adopted my suggestion of a built-in button hole in the napkins. I like the French practice of putting napkins under the chin to shield the coat or shirt from spillings.

So nod, shave on plane, eat and the day passed by. There's no place like Maggie. Good to be home.

Bob Mooney elected in Nantucket; anxious to fix breakfast tomorrow and thus be in soft routine of 2 Fifth.

As a whole, the trip was worthwhile.

Monday, November 21

Back to a foot-high stack of mail which Paula had left at home, and another foot or more at the office. Kept girls busy giving answer.

Peter Beer advises that a group of lawyers have offered services to the New Orleans School Board in the integration mess. Most gratifying—and this may be beginning of some leadership in that sorely-troubled town. On the theory of combatting un-Americanism they should try to get chairmen of House and Senate Committees to come down, tenderly take the hand of one of the four-year-old Negro students and escort the lads into their schools.

Worked all day, dropped in at Joan's and saw Arlene, an expert soon in sign language, and Steffie who is teaching her all day.

For dinner Edna and good talk on Israel from which land she has returned. Like old times.

Joan drops in at midnight—more cheerful than she has been in a long time. Once more she takes life as an adventure.

The girls in the office have asked me to give a travel talk on the West and Southwest as I do after returning from other foreign cultures.

Tuesday, November 22

Olin Stephens in to talk New Horizon.[200] He's a shy painter and creator of sail boats. It's too bad he ever has to touch the messy realms of commerce. I should have thought that his keels would move through water in leisurely fashion. But no

[200] Class of sailboat.

—he is a hot-rod expert of the sea, mad about the perfections of speed.

More dictating, more clients, more rush, hectic—without a calm moment.

Home—napped after dinner and to bed early after reading British magazines *Listener* and *Encounter*, and Jack Fischer in *Harper's*.

Friday, November 25

At Overseas Press Club with Ray Harwood—good mind and informed on business end of publishing business. In the main the author-editorial end attracts the best brains away from the distribution of books. It's a pity, for each title is, in a way, a separate business. Few consumers ask for a Harper or a Knopf publication imprint. This creates a supreme burden—in fact, more than half of the books sent out by publishers are in packages of five or less. So once more I hammer my hobbyhorse: Why is postage on books three or four times as high as for the same weight magazines? Why any postage on international flow of books? Why any tariff on paper for books when newsprint comes in free? We discussed discrimination against knowledge in hard covers—all amusing, but to no avail until we find a Leader, one person with a sense of mission in favor of books.

Home to dinner—relaxed although most of the leaves have fallen from most of the trees outside our window.

Maggie tells me "canard" comes from French "duck"—flying around, as a false report; and to "half-sell a duck" (a French expression) is "not to sell at all"—hence extravagant, or absurd story.

Read article about R. H. Tawney—who is 80 this month.

I am in his debt, having read *Sickness of an Acquisitive Society* at, for me, the impressionable moment.

Saturday and Sunday, November 26 and 27

Events of pleasant contours occurred. Harvard Club party of Marc Friedlaender—met a spark-eyed chemist; saw movie *Savage Eye*—stark and futile, since producers had nothing but yen to snap pictures, and no philosophy about the matrix of the film, loneliness; coffee with Stevenson family of Keystone fame—interested in stern symbols created for two attractive daughters; saw Dr. Becque of N.Y.U. re dance program. Touched by retirement of Helen Masten who was a storyteller for children at N.Y. Public Library for thirty-eight years —a story worthy of more space than the undaring report of the President's Committee on National Goals, a shockingly inadequate report of frightened men who did not know that dreams and ideals make history—a report that will do major harm; excited when Penelope, just back in town, tells me of chickens, bred from same line, which have a complete resistance to leukemia-like cancer. We also discussed cross-breeding and the Churk—a cross between turkey and chicken. I'm told only three are alive but for science in man's grasp, one of anything is enough—once is the test. Man can make one, he can make more. And man once learning how to make a bit more brain, must have the power to keep on making more and more mind.

But the days are sombre. The blows that come to us are of our own making. They hurt and cut deep, at least until we admit error, express regret for a fleeting second, learn from regret, and promptly forget it—using it only as a springboard for nonrepetition.

Monday, November 28

Lunch with Eddie—relaxed, profitable and too rare. Received from Sir Allen Lane [201] a copy of his first edition of *Lady Chatterley* inscribed by Allen and all his barristers and solicitors. Happy to have been of some slight help. Shipped to University of Texas my *Ulysses* collection. Newman,[202] my favorite appraiser, did do a handsome job of boxing, and so forth.

Tuesday, November 29

Good news—Appeals Court reverses Apalachin conviction. Good because there was no evidence of guilt, and the jury had convicted because the press and TV were out for blood. Called tops of Bar Association of City—here is a chance for lawyers to lead the people. Sure nothing will happen. No fire in bellies of lawyers.

Berkshire *Eagle* review of *Touch Wood* calls me Irreverent Legal Gadfly. Maybe true as to Legal and Gadfly—but I revere freedom and lack of cant.

Rundquist for lunch to see if I can help support Kennedy, our Police Commissioner, who is bait of press. He will be driven out of office by mass media. Since our government is one of separation of functions, the press is acutely important in resolving the public mind. Less needed in England where the Parliamentary system prevails.

Went to plastic expert to get ear pieces made to fit me and a hearing aid. My vanity is not a factor. But won't clients react less warmly? As it is, I hear all I want and all I need,

[201] Of Penguin Books.
[202] Ralph Newman of Chicago, literary appraiser, Lincolniana collector.

except for a few voices—all feminine, pitched at my poorer wave lengths.

Wednesday, November 30

Penelope tells me that male babies in Liberia are left in fields to die. In India it is the female infants that are liabilities. Both practices derive from same convention, the dower system. In India parents figure that females can only be got rid of by paying dower, which puts family in hock to village banker. In Liberia the males are worthless because they do not bring dower to parents. It's an odd world with people treated as pawns. But better than Angola which, as much of Africa, is still using slavery as a way of life.

Welthy Fisher in to see me about her great educational program for India. She'll not go places in Washington because she is seeking thousands instead of millions of dollars.

December

Thursday, December 1

An inquiring medico from Philadelphia, Walter Ballinger, came to town and I shifted lunch date with attractive dame to get his thinking. He's troubled about his profession and, among other subjects, we discussed the tawdry increase of suits for malpractice. A real financial burden on the profession, not to mention blackmail implications on reputation through irresponsible press that loves hurts and dirt.

Pat Knopf [203] in and talked distribution of books. Some day I'd like to see a study: books which had enthusiastic approval of all critics but still failed to be best sellers, and books which are on the best seller lists and gathered slight, if any, encomiums from reviewers.

[203] Alfred A. Knopf, Jr., partner, Atheneum Publishers.

Home early to meet with Anna Kross and Dave Jones. As dedicated correction officials they are worried that we do so little with the antisocials who troop through police courts and jails—to be returned, incapacitated to live *conveniently* with their neighbors. Anna has a bellyful of fire. How she holds her high job I can't fathom.

For dinner, the Frank Samuels [204] family. Chitchat except for the enthusiasm of the young barrister, Jim Hirsch.

Weather gets zippy and I wear a coat for the first time. What magnificent autumn we have enjoyed.

Friday, Saturday and Sunday, December 2, 3 and 4

Friday was a day of many events, but still I felt blasé, which for me is not anything like being bored. I'm never bored by myself or with my family, never with events, scenery or nature's views or happenings—only by men and women or, at times, ill-mannered children.

Life poured in on me—fitted for ear pieces for eye glass hearing aid; art exhibit at City and Country School, where met the E.S.G.'s [205] and the Eddie Kuhs [206]—all coming home with us for a drink. A psychoanalyst visitor told new approach to the Hiss mystery. Saw a lovable child on a bus, a kid in love—her eyes were globes burning with love, adoration and affection—in love as only a child can be—but the object was not a person, not an animal, but a book. Picked up Lena L. for walk and coffee back at 2 Fifth; dinner at a quiet Armenian restaurant, the Dardanelles on University Place; rich day with Maggie, her birthday. Presents and all the frills befitting our age and era—with overeating at Mag's to cele-

[204] Brother-in-law.
[205] The Eddie Greenbaums.
[206] Old friend from college days.

brate with the Goldies. *Herald Tribune* mentions *Touch Wood* as one of the memorable books of 1960. Lunch with publisher Watts and agree to do with Alan S. the Lawyers Book in his series of occupations—50,000 words, good advance, and with dignified associates—Margaret Mead and others. Some other time of year this event alone would have been a headline in my life.

The week end with my kind of weather, with double crostic, with potato pancakes—with much of big and small, no peaks, no valleys—just living.

Monday, December 5

Mail flows in on *Touch Wood*. One card reads, "No Fool Like an Old Fool." Of all my partners only three ever mentioned the book, even though they, I know, sent out copies as presents. Do I scare them? Or did they dislike it? Or were they sore they were left out of the volume by editor? Talked to secretaries about trip to alien lands such as Alabama, New Orleans, Texas and no-culture Los Angeles. All were interested and several wrote me notes. I'm touched when people take out a minute to be generous in feeling—as in this letter: "Thanks so much for the luncheon—you have a rare talent for teaching valuable things while seeming only to entertain. Everything you touched on really taught us a lesson—you made it look so easy to tear down the obvious with one hand and build up the unsuspected truth with the other. But I know it's not easy. Thanks again."

Tuesday, December 6

Event: federal tax agent bores me for hours—it's quite un-British and indecent. Imbedded in our mores is acceptance of the theory that the agent must find something—so tax-payers decide doubts in agent's favor and are ready to bargain. I've tried both techniques, and honor doesn't pay off.

An engineer is examining the office. They say, "to tighten up the operation." This means: how can we cut out the defects of bigness?

Lunch with Lael W.—both chatter at each other with gaiety. Happy she is busy at her craft.

Police Commissioner and George Rundquist at 2 Fifth in afternoon to discuss policy proposals I have developed. How far should the State license barbers, guns, pool rooms, taxi drivers? Should police be the contact in all cases between State and citizen? Should we adopt British police standards re dual jobs—called moonlighting—or conflicts of interest? I'm starting to wonder whether "Chief" is a title or a position with power—à la Edgar Hoover.

To AIGA dinner—met again with pleasure Executive Vice President of McGraw-Hill and Charles F. Bound, Vice President of Morgan's. Talks were frightening—as if mergers were ineluctable. I'm not for or against mergers—each case is an *ad hoc* decision. Blew my top after a question was directed to me. One speaker analogized mergers of trucking concerns to those of book companies!

Maggie recalls that on the day before Pearl Harbor E. R.[207] and H. A. W.[208] and Jimmy Marshall [209] were at our home for tea. All calm. The next day I had set up a lunch at the White House. I called up—should it be called off? Oh, no. Mrs. R. carried on with Mary Lasker and others. I recall seeing Francis Biddle in the hall upstairs—and his face, loaded with trouble, remains a forbidding picture.

Life goes on.

[207] Eleanor Roosevelt.
[208] Henry A. Wallace.
[209] Lawyer, former President of N.Y. Board of Education.

Thursday, December 8

At home Maggie explains origin of word "nepotism"—Italian *nepote,* nephew. The opportunities for advancement by being the Pope's nephews. Which, I add, probably meant being an illegitimate son called a nephew.

Called in on a circus—called a law suit—brought by the Corporation Counsel of the City, based on affidavits of the county prosecutors and Chief of Police, against a score of publishers (unrelated to each other), a mass of distributors and a hundred or so newsstand gentry—dealers in girlie magazines. No sadism, such as makes fortunes for daily newspapers and TV networks, and no charge of conspiracy among the competing publishers. It's as if one hundred pickpockets who picked the pockets of one hundred different people were joined in one trial. Or a hundred tax evaders. What are we coming to? The Apalachin trial was a travesty and needed the spanking reversal which it got if we were to preserve due process. But now a new public racket has been begun by law enforcement officials.

Maggie to ballet and I to OPC where I picked up comparative strangers—for wine and steak sandwich dinner.

Friday, December 9

Spoke at Copyright Society at Lotos Club on Russian situation. Did very badly—never able to get to nonroving minds of specialists, and these were all specialists. I believe that specialization is antagonistic to social inventions. No bookkeeper can invent a new triple-entry system—only a fringe improvement on double-entry.

How To Make is in rehearsal—must go and watch it.

265

Bill Astor sends a card to Atheneum boosting *Touch Wood*.

Wrote H. S. T. for a Long Island lawyer who is giving a dinner for Democrats, and wants to recapture Lincoln for his party. H. S. T. writes an answer of a good historian:

I appreciated very much yours of November 28th and the enclosed letter from George Soll.

I think you had better tell Mr. Soll that Abraham Lincoln was a Whig and when he was in Congress he was against everything that the Democrats wanted. He was nominated on the Republican Ticket in 1860 in Chicago and then when he found there were a great many Union Democrats who did not want to secede from the Union he had a convention held in Baltimore known as the American Union and he and Andrew Johnson were nominated on that ticket. Then after Lincoln was shot every effort was made by the radical Republicans to discredit Andrew Johnson, which they almost succeeded in doing.

I don't see any reason for trying to bring Lincoln into the Democratic Party. The Republicans have always used him as the head of their Party.

Sincerely yours,
HARRY S TRUMAN

Home for dinner. Sad at further breach in understanding between U.S. and Canada. How clumsy can we get? I can't wait for the heirs of Dulles to get the hell out of Washington so that our Republic can return to the good will which proceeds from diplomacy as compared to confusions of publicity. Was it not Jefferson who inserted in the Declaration of Independence the idea that we and Great Britain ". . . could also have been great and together forever"? So also Canada which, if the roads had been passable in the 1780's, would have been our fourteenth state.

Monday, December 12

After a loving autumn, New York and the entire seaboard was visited by heavy snow and gale-force winds. This morning snow banks on highways but no flakes left on the branches of our trees except the main stems. Off to office—excited by this minor challenge—knowing that all whom I would meet would be proud and elated too. Like the bank holiday of the Hoover depression when everyone rose to the occasion, lending money to strangers whose unrecognized dollars or pennies, no one could guess which, were beyond use. Man trusts man in an emergency. Today women helped women over piles of snow, young men gave up seats in buses to young or old women. The species becomes polite and cheerful and proud of living. All except the bus drivers—for they continue their inconsiderate attitudes even when the bus is not crowded and when all folk are willing to forgive past discourtesies. A great day to witness mankind in love.

At office only a few show up, but those who do beam with superiority—"We made it."

Then to Joan's on the way home to give Steffie an adding machine—premature and inadequate as most toys made for young minds. Took home other science equipment for Kathie and Nick. No one is too young to behold some little bit of a magnificent miracle of nature. So witnessed a human miracle —Churchill on TV. Sometime in history, man makes institutions but at other stages institutions make men.

Kennedy shows up well in his appointments. I think he intends to be the President—not like Ike who, ignorant of civilian problems, looked to George Humphries and Foster Dulles to take over the reins.

Tuesday, December 13

Friendliness continues in our city. I grabbed a cab—a young gal was waiting. I asked her to share, and when she got out I suggested she give the driver fifty cents as an extra tip and I'd pay the meter. The driver refused to accept the coin, saying, "Money isn't everything in life." So if we only had more havoc, man would live with the moral equivalent he discovers and uses in such profligate fashion during a war.

At dinner Judge Burton and Ralph Newman—to discuss the confusions of the librarians, manuscript collectors, and all interested in the perpetuation and spread of knowledge—whether written, typed or printed. Storm kept others from joining us. It has been urged that all letters are written at writer's peril—if the receiver may not only exhibit at a library, but publish for royalty profits. We need a vast amount of new thinking by the experts, with the aid of nonspecialists.

Nantucket item. A couple divorced fifty-eight years ago—each remarrying in meanwhile, each losing spouse by death—have just remarried. What a bond—or is it regrets, or is it loneliness? Aren't men and women odd, even at eighty-three and eighty-four years of age?

Thursday, December 15

Dinner at Goldies'—a banquet with Joan's best chinaware, tablecloth and fittings. Occasions such as this carry a different importance for deaf people than for others. It seems to make up for debits such as opera, dancing, concerts and the like denied to them. Even talkie movies are the equivalent of the old silent films.

For lunch, Poppy Cannon, just back from Nigeria and

Ghana and much to tell. She indicated talks with head officials about my fanatic desire for literacy and education by mass media. Particularly where, as in these lands, there is no one overriding language. Rather three languages and dozens of dialects. So the Head of State cannot be understood if he talks to his people—as in India where nearly 100 million people are not in language communication range of Nehru.

Friday, December 16

Loafed late what with slush on the highways. Busy at office —sent new Secretary of Labor letter of suggestions, lunch with Cass and his cohorts to discuss planned parenthood and the difficulties of the Catholic Church. How few people know Catholic position that inadequate housing is an indication for limitation of family.

Home with ties and goodies and cards received for holidays. Alan and Paula to dinner. Good talk in a world where I find so few people with a single new idea or even a query.

Saturday, December 17

Saturday was a pilgrimage to Westchester for a family party at Frank and Edith Samuels'. About thirty people for lunch, a party that Joan loved. As Maggie said, she would have enjoyed Natchez, where family gatherings were central in people's lives—people less interested in the solar spaces, the planet, Europe, or even the adjacent state, than in the lives of intimates.

In evening to the Harris' for another party—M. tired and retired at about 10 P.M., and I stayed until brownish hour of 3 A.M. All young folk and I liked them. They raise their voices in argument. They have more heat than dignity. A group from *The New York Times* agreed that it is so far out in front that its problems become: What will keep its reporters on their toes? Will there not be a temptation to lower standards to gain quantity? What instruments can be devised to take the place of competition—not from the orgy press like the *Post,* or from the bewildered such as the well-written and even more courageous *Tribune,* or the shabby *News* and Hearst papers, but from the areas of sobriety? Not easy to be in a race and be so far ahead that there is no danger of being overtaken and no need to turn one's head to look for the nearest runner.

Sunday, December 18

Felt lousy—watery eyes and nose, rough trachea—so didn't get out of pajamas all day. Nicholas came up and I gave him a microscope—not toy, but real size. I deplore the ones used for Christmas presents given to kids. Waste of money, soon broken, and seldom hold interest beyond the first thrill of a "new" possession. He seemed delighted.

Then toyed with items Penelope gave me to ponder in field of science. Why is uterine cancer curable? Who can tell me secrets such as: Why do more male than female sea urchins get born if water is warm? What are uses of noninflammable rubber—still resilient at 60° below zero? Perhaps on non-inflammable airplanes or cars? At last, a machine into which I can speak ten words and have them come out on tape in readable form. The answer to the communication problems of Joan and Irving. Silicon solar cells convert light into energy—so maybe moving pictures for teaching literacy in lands where there is no gas or water power. Penelope tells me that Louis Braille started his writing for the blind by driving nails into a board.

And so I mused—disturbed that the press thinks such ideas are less attractive to readers than a murder case or air accident.

Monday, December 19

Increasingly interested in Darvas case, which isn't a case. The highest law officer of the state, the Attorney General, is investigating a book. No charges, no indictment, no bill of particulars—just the use of press and TV and radio by the Attorney General. And all I meet have found the author and publisher guilty of a fraud. Thus do we lose not only justice, but a sense of justice, until in time—and the time will come—when we also lose faith in a free press and cynicism destroys our first amendment. Oddly enough, the core of this evil backtalks on itself. The Attorney General investigates an untruthful book, under the law—that very same law that exempts newspapers and magazines and gives them the legal green light to defraud the public as to stock market movements. Only books are vulnerable—lawyers, stock exchange firms and the daily press received exemptions in the new law.

Tuesday, December 20

Lunch with Bass, energetic barrister for Darvas. Good to see some young lawyers who are not ashamed of outrage and do not try to hide it.

Worked on new reply in Birth Control case—since State of Connecticut claims legislation is valid on moral grounds. Here I lose them. What line of morals is there between con-

tinence, withdrawal, rhythm spotting or calendars, the pill—
all approved by the Catholic Church, and the diaphragm
approved by the U.S. Medical Health Service.

Wednesday, December 21

At home in evening, read Bohn in *New Leader* and thrilled
to find his piece on *Touch Wood*. I haven't seen Bill Bohn for
years but his review gave me a real holiday feeling. Maybe
I'm a misplaced person, as he says. I'll write him to come
along with me to live in Florence during the time of the
Medicis, or in Virginia with Jefferson and Madison. In the
forward direction—well, who can pick the site of his own
distant Utopia, or the date?